The Love We Lost

How to Reconnect and Rebuild Your Relationship

Elizabeth Lucas-Afolalu
Award-Winning Author

THE LOVE WE LOST
How to Reconnect and
Rebuild Your Relationship

Copyright © 2020 by Elizabeth Lucas-Afolalu

ISBN: 978-1-8380552-0-2

LEGAL DISCLAIMER

This book is designed to inspire and motivate readers and also to provide useful information. It is sold with the understanding that the publisher is not engaged to render any type of professional counselling, psychological, legal, or any other kind of professional advice. The content of each article is the sole expression and opinion of its author, and not necessarily that of the publisher. No warranties or guarantees are expressed or implied by the publisher's choice to include any of the content in this volume. Neither the publisher nor the individual author shall be liable for any physical, psychological, emotional, financial, or commercial damages, including, but not limited to, special, incidental, consequential or other damages. Our views and rights are the same: You are responsible for your own choices, actions, and results. Although the author and publisher have made every effort to ensure that the information in this book was correct at press time, the author and publisher do not assume and hereby disclaim any liability to any party for any loss, damage, or disruption caused by errors or omissions, whether such errors or omissions result from negligence, accident, or any other cause.

Published by:
TOKMEZ PUBLISHING
ESSEX, UNITED KINGDOM

Table of the contents

Book Preface

ACKNOWLEDGEMENTS

DEDICATION

TESTIMONIALS

Chapter 1: Introduction

Chapter 2: Let talk about Love itself

Chapter 3: Q & A of love and relationship

Chapter 4: The truth about love

Chapter 5: Forgiveness

Chapter 6: Managing Emotions

Chapter 7: Communication is the Key

Chapter 8: Techniques to help you forgive

Chapter 9: The Strategy of Love

Chapter 10: Love Quotes

About the Author

The Love We Lost

TESTIMONIALS

"Elizabeth Lucas-Afolalu in her book 'The Love We Lost' share her vast experience over a number of year with great tips and advice for you the Reader to enhance your Relationships. Her previous books have touched the lives of many and it is her wish to do the same for you with Love in this book".
Philip Chan – 7 Times Award Winning Author Aka 10 Seconds Maths Expert and Confidence Life Coach

"Elizabeth Lucas-Afolalu, the Author of this book "The Love We Lost" is an inspirational Speaker, a Motivator and she determined to do what is right and share her wisdom to the world. This attributes has really helped her in all ramification of life endeavour. She is a woman of little words but contain facts and truth. Among her peer groups, she is very respected and diligent in whatever she does. Elizabeth is a lovely woman who practices what she belief and say. This is A Must Book for everyone to read. This book brings experiences, stories, reality, awareness, principles and wisdom. There was joy and love that nothing on this earth could give me and that I can relate with this book. No matter how far I have drifted my relationship, the memory of that joy and love always draws me back. I wish everyone get to experience this love as I have experienced it for the past 29 years in my marital life. Well done on completing this amazing book about love and forgiveness and reconnecting the family."
Deacon Olufemi Lucas-Afolalu JP, Mentor, speaker, Motivator and Leader

"Elizabeth has a way of writing that touches your soul. Her message is clear and concise, as she guides us through what the gift of love means and how we can restore and maintain it. Using her unique challenges and

her perspective on the teachings of God, she offers deep insight that can only be realised and expressed through living the experience and overcoming. This is why the book is so necessary and special and which is why I highly recommend investing in this guidebook on love. This book can be read at any time; to prepare yourself for new love, to help you through challenges with your current love, and to also think about past love and potentially restoring what you lost through misunderstanding and lack of direction. This is a thoroughly enjoyable read; Elizabeth makes learning about love accessible to all".
Laura Amherst, Chief Editor for DVG and the Soveriegn Magazine.

Book Preface

One of My Mission's is to support Youths, Women, Families, individually, locally and internationally, offline and online through media and resources, gifts, products, workshops, seminars and speaking engagements to help them to:
- Change their Mind-set
- Discover, develop, and demonstrate their gift
- Build deeper relationship and maintain
- Restore and reconnect relationship and families
- Manage their emotions and be free and be happy
- Learn to forgive themselves and others
- Learn to love them and love others
- Create Roadmap for the youths for the future

ACKNOWLEDGEMENTS

My gratitude to Almighty God who has given me this assignment and opportunity to share my inspirational Nuggets of Wisdom to the world

My gratitude also goes to:

Pastor Matthew Ashimolowo who through his tiredness teachings on relationship and success, I have learnt from. My Mentors, Friends, Dream Helpers who have motivated me to achieve and write this book, to many people whom I've learnt a lot from: Phillip Chan, Myles Munroe, Jim Rohn, Mensah Otabil, Les Brown, Joyce Meyer, Mama Veronica Tan, Mirela Sula, John Maxwell, Mike Murdock, Tony Robbins, Bob Proctor, Andy Harrington, Raymond Aaron, TD Jakes, Michele Obama, Oprah Winfrey, for their series of motivation that has kept me and educated me through their seminars, workshops, books, audio and other resources.

Mrs Laura Amherst – my Amazing Proof-reader/Editor for her tiredness hardwork, very efficient and my Book Designer – Mr Waqas Ahmed for his eye-catching book cover.

My gratitude to My Mother – Mrs S.O. Akintonde, my confidant, my adviser, mentor, who taught me and showed me the moral values and how to be contented, focus, humble myself, be grateful, treat and respect people and to become a woman of excellence.

My gratitude to my relationship mentor Mrs Florence Awosoga for her inspiration and wisdom. She gave me my lessons of love and relationship, stood by me during my wedding ceremony, and continues to support me till today; she opened her door for me to learn what is mean to love at my early age,

My loving and caring husband, my great wonderful children, for the opportunity given to me to use them as my platform to experiment and exhibit love and to many friends and relatives that has given me opportunity to experience, to learn and grow stronger for years.

Also, all of you spending time reading this book and trusting in me to motivate and inspire you and start believing in yourself that Yes, you can forgive and love again, you can reconnect and rebuild your relationships again because all things are possible.

DEDICATION

I dedicate this book to:
My husband (aka LOVE), and my wonderful children

I dedicate this book to you that is reading this book because I believe you are searching for answers about the love we lost.

The Love We Lost

CHAPTER ONE

INTRODUCTION

How many of you have seen yourselves in a situation of lost love, and said to yourself, you cannot or will not ever love again?

How many of you have felt disappointed and come to the conclusion that there is no such thing as love?

What is the meaning of love anyway? And what goes wrong in love?

How do we deal with other people's opinions, comparisons, criticisms and judgments?

Do you want to know the five secrets of overcoming flesh and lust?

Finally, do you want to learn how to forgive, communicate, love again, reconnect, restore, and rebuild trust?

I will be sharing in this book, how to build, maintain, recover and restore love with trust in our relationship. I have many more answers to some of the interesting questions we have about these topics.

Everyone has suffered some sort of emotional hurt through the words or actions of another. Experiencing this hurt is completely natural, but sometimes the hurt lasts longer than it needs to. This makes it harder to be happy and, if we can't let go and move on, it can ruin relationships. Someone that will never forgive is someone destined to be alone. In every challenge of life, there are always storms, and there are ways to come out of those storms, situations are not permanent, there is always movement, however, storms force you to change and become stronger and renewed.

Many people have become used to hiding their emotions. They allow them to govern their lives uncontrollably, which leads to many unresolved conflicts, both internal and external, which sends mixed messages to the people around them and his creates numerous issues waiting to be resolved. The person in touch with their emotions, and who knows how to detach from them, control and understand them, is viewed as stable, professional and reliable. And they really are, because they don't allow emotions to rule their lives.

I developed a strength within myself when I learnt that forgiving someone does not mean it "didn't happen." Forgiveness doesn't necessarily resume trust; we have to do our part toward reconciliation. I know through experience (both past and present-day) –

We can choose to forgive and allow that to work within our hearts.

We can cut off every place where anger, hurt, bitterness, and fearful thoughts of self-pity or self-righteousness have risen up in us.

We can find ourselves free of all emotional attachment to it, we even forget it, or it can become nothing more than a memory to us.

We can bless those who have injured us with a sincere heart. We may even be willing to return to the relationship we once had and build what God intended to build the first time around.

The miracle of healing requires your Forgiveness; to yourself and others. Let go, let them go, and your miracle can come in. Forgiveness supports you in turning your back to bitterness. I like the quote, "Forgiveness is giving up all hope of a bitter past." If you have a regret about something you've done, use this moment to forgive yourself. If you have resentment against someone else, use this time to forgive him or her. Things don't always go as planned. Learn to forgive and forgive quickly. It will reflect in your emotions and give you peace, joy and success.

Some of the elements that lead to a breakdown in relationships (including mental, emotional and physical abuse) include:
- Emotional breakdowns
- General frustrations/ and anger issues.
- The anxiety of the unknowns in life.
- Insecurities
- Inferiority complexes
- Disappointments
- Discouragements
- Partners being unfaithful
- Influence of family and friends
- Substance misuse

I believe there are solutions to these issues in a relationship but first things first. We should have open, honest communication, where both parties can admit where they may have problems; and from that point, help should be sought. This could be in the form of Professional counselling; Pastoral counselling; Prayer; Support from friends; deliverance. Even the willingness to help others with our testimonies can be profoundly healing.

With God, all things are possible, and there is nothing too difficult for God. Remember life can be short, life can be hard sometimes, it is not comfortable nor is it easy if we have many problems on our minds. We have got to take one day at a time. To add analogies, Rome was not built in a day, and it takes patience to cook a delicious soup.

The Love We Lost

If we persevere, the universe will make sure we see that no matter how far, God travels with us in all directions. This is so as we may overcome all of our trials, tribulations and challenges in life. The sea may be rough, but it is possible to be fulfilled and be successful in life, and all things are possible.

Sometimes we can get involved in blame games.
We may blame many other people, including parents, the government, criminals, cheating spouses, rebellious children, social services. But when we blame people, we do not take responsibility for ourselves. Many charities, community groups and religious leaders work hard to find solutions to pressing social issues. However, this is made harder if individually and collectively, we try to push the main problem aside.

There is no point dealing with the problem from the surface or from the top, we must understand the root of the issue. We must recognise it is an intergenerational problem. The earlier we can intervene and provide assistance, the better chance we have of helping our men, women and children. However, allow us to begin with individuals.

I am going to share a part of my life experience briefly to illuminate what I am trying to explain.

My life experience was full of shame, abandonment, rejection and isolation. I have been homeless at times and felt lonely in crowds; as if I were crying into the wilderness. I was emotionally, physically, sexually and verbally abused. This has resulted in me having very low self-esteem, a lack of confidence, rejection anxiety, frustration, and issues with denial.

I have attempted suicide several times. I was afraid to speak out, share my inner world with others. I was always pleasing others and going out of my way, but in the process, I was neglecting myself. I struggled to give and receive love.

The question here is: how can a person love others if they don't love themselves?

I was used and dumped in the name of love and lost my identity in the process. I was raped, tricked, and poorly treated. I came to believe all the negative words said to me throughout the years, and I eventually adopted them for myself, which led to my downfall. I had a lot of anxiety and was afraid to stand up in front of people or to speak out in public. Through all the mistreatment, I held onto my anger.

I was afraid it would continue before I got married. I wanted to stay single to focus on my life, to serve God and travel all over the world to share his greatness. Did that work? Oh no.

I entered into my marriage with emotional trauma, and instead of it getting better, it got worse. We both went through everything you can think of; every storm, every crisis. We both raised children without a sense of belonging, and I became depressed, suicidal and harboured a lot of self-hatred. I could not receive love and compliments, and I found myself always supporting others before myself, believing that things would get better later. I became a perfectionist, defensive, presumptuous, controlling and negative, and not the compassionate person that I wanted to be. I gradually began to outgrow these issues with the help of my pastor, who was constantly teaching me how to persevere and grow. Still, I didn't feel I was making enough progress. I studied everything in the bible on love and prayer and was getting a better understanding. Most of all, I sought wisdom and to be endowed with more patience.

We overcame our struggles; we are still standing and loving one another. I have learnt that with love, we can do anything and that everything happens for a reason. I realised that situations in my life were the platforms I needed to experiment and experience, and turn negativity into positivity.

The Love We Lost

If a person does not seek help and ask they can't receive it. Suffering in silence is not the way forward, and the situation can become much worse unless a person reaches out. Our lives and journeys are our priority, as when we develop other elements in our life will naturally fall into place. We must remember we cannot change others, but only change our responses and make the decisions for our lives.

How did I constantly bounce back, recover and reconnect? I recognised I had problems and that the challenges were overwhelming me, day and night. I knew the only person that could sav, me, deliver and guide me through is God himself, and I knew where to go to seek for help.

I sought the Highest God, and I was determined to follow his directions. In the depths of my heart, the same question arose in me: How can you love others if you don't love yourself? One day, I said to myself, enough is enough. It is my responsibility to change things around and be what God created me to be. Other people's opinions of me will not stop me. With the love and help of Jesus who came into my life, I was able to do this.

You might be asking, how did Jesus change my life?

When I was at the lowest point in my life, I cried out to the invincible Father, the Almighty God, to save me. I looked for love from the Father of Fathers.

I asked him to sustain me and help me find the best way to serve him and love others. I wanted him to show me the ways to forgive myself and forgive others.
I surrendered myself and welcomed Jesus Christ as my Lord and my saviour, my advocate and mentor.

I knew that Jesus is the only one that can save me, love me and care for me. I asked for his strength and wisdom to face the reality of my life; for wisdom and grace and the power to be happy.

To my surprise, God answered my prayers, and I began to find new friends in God's Kingdom. I began to walk with God, and God walked with me. He directed me and connected me. He disciplined me, guiding all my footsteps. With Jesus' strength and help, I grew from strength to strength, inspiring people and sharing love and hope with them.

I went through all kinds of abuse, but I was still standing and still doing well. I learnt that Jesus died so that I could be saved. I believe in loving my neighbour as myself, and I can do all things through Christ who gives me strength, and a deep calling of mine was to become an evangelist. I wanted to preach the gospel and share the good news of our Lord Jesus Christ.

Though I knew Jesus could set people free, I did not realise that Jesus my coach, mentor, and teacher was taking me on a journey where I would learn what love is and how to forgive. Jesus was taking me on a journey where I would learn how to be humble and patient; where I would understand people and be able to support them. I was embarking on a great journey.

When you don't understand the main reason why people behave in a certain way, it can affect relationships, and love may be lost.

In my own personal experience, I found myself in a situation where I had nearly lost all hope, and I had to make decisions about my life. My relationships were crumbling around me, and I didn't know what to do anymore.

Have you found yourself in a situation where you've given all your love to certain people, and they throw your love in the trash? Have you ever found yourself trying as hard as you can for a person to still not value you? Have you ever found yourself loving the wrong person?

The Love We Lost

Have you ever found yourself at a crossroads where you wonder if the relationship is worth trying harder for or if you should just give up?

I went to many seminars, meetings, counselling sessions. I read many books and watched many videos; but still found myself unsatisfied and on the verge of believing that nothing would work for me.

I used to have counselling sessions with my pastor, and he tirelessly taught me about relationships. He taught me about using SWOT analysis to make sense of situations I found myself in with people.

I was young, and it wasn't until I studied the same concept in Business and management for it to all make sense.

I realised that we can use this same analysis to understand ourselves and to understand other people that we love.

SWOT stands for strength, weakness, opportunity and threat. An added part is that we can understand our similarities and differences and learn how to embrace our imperfection and celebrate one another.

In terms of helping my romantic relationships, I read many books which helped me to understand that women and men have differences. These differences range from communications, emotions, and problem-solving.

I learnt how to communicate effectively; at the right times with the right tonality and gestures. I learnt when to speak and when to keep quiet and at what point to stop talking to avoid unnecessary arguments. I began to understand my boundaries and appreciate and embrace my commitment to my partner. I developed the courage to press forward, stay in the relationship and deal with the situation with God's wisdom. I learnt how to express myself which lead to a much better connection.

Honesty, integrity, openness, trust and forgiveness, combined with decision making, determination and discipline of mind, body and soul, developed in me the necessary dedication that I needed to continue in healthy ways and make progress.

One of the events that I attended was the Power to Achieve weekend with Andy Harrington as the keynote speaker. He drew my attention to the awareness of coping mechanisms. He explained to me that all of us have experienced moments of emotional pain and of course, it's natural to want to avoid those situations happening all over again.

As a result, we can develop coping mechanisms whenever we feel stressed or challenged. These coping mechanisms cause us to experience the 3 Ds:

- DELAY the inevitability of change.
- DENY that there is something that's not quite right in our world.
- DISTRACTION from the reality that our lives are not the way we want them to be.

He explained further that there are many types of coping behaviours, but they can be easily summed up as stemming from one of 4 character types which he called the shadow selves:
- The Controller (dominates);
- The Pleaser (is dominated);
- The Analyser (retreats in their head) and;
- The Busy Keeper (juggles situations)

He taught me to turn away from these shadow aspects of self to find the warrior within that can love, joke and focus on wisdom.

From this, I developed a much better understanding of myself, which has been useful in understanding others as well. This has helped me create better relationships and better behaviours.

To learn more about these concepts and gain more insight and wisdom, I suggest reading Andy's book "Passion to Profit".

Throughout this process, I started looking at people and treating them differently; especially my husband.

I started to look at our relationship from a different angle, and I learnt to embrace our imperfections and differences. I fully grasped that I can only change myself. I started to be open to the idea that by helping, loving and improving myself and my actions, I might influence my husband in positive ways. And I can conclude that it works!

I started speaking the positive words that I include below to him:

Wise words to My Love

You are carrying the special and greatest anointing of God. I'm grateful to God. You are the best man for me, you are a man of honour, you are a man of God and A true leader, you are blessed and highly favoured.

A man that finds a wife finds a good thing and has obtained favour from God and ith this ordained union, God blesses us with a handsome, intelligent, hardworking, strong, clever and very focused Son; and a beautiful, creative, smart, Solid, diligent and focused Daughter.

They are our champions, our Eagles, and our Seeds. The gift of God has added signs and wonders that are manifesting in their lives. I'm grateful to God that you are my husband, the bone of my bone, and the flesh of my flesh. My friend, you are my mirror, My mentor, my coach, my strength and my spokesman.

It's so easy, enjoyable and wonderful to be behind you because I trust you, believe in you, honour you and love you.

The Love We Lost

I look into your eyes every day, and I thank God as I watch the way you faithfully serve him, and I am in constant admiration.

The fear of The Lord is the beginning of wisdom, and you are full of God's wisdom. You are so funny, You make me laugh and make others laugh, and even during our challenges we laughed together.

When our Love and relationship is tested, we still stand by God's grace, and when our faith is challenged, we again trust God together. Grace sustains us. Your prayer lifestyle at home gave me assurance that our latter rain will be better than our former rain.

God will do a new thing in us, and delay is not denial. Arises and Shine, for the light, has come and the glory of The Lord has risen inside you. Keep standing, keep striving, Keep declaring, Keep singing, keep shining, Keep laughing, Keep rejoicing, and keep dancing.

MICRO JOURNAL

MICRO JOURNAL

Dates	

CHAPTER 2

LET'S TALK ABOUT LOVE

If we all loved just a little bit more, the world would be a better place!

In this chapter, I focus on what love IS: the overarching principles and what it really means.

I include the different types of love and how it manifests in our daily lives.

I have written most of this information in a bullet point format to make the information easier to digest.

I focus on how love transforms over time, and I have included notes on self-love and God's all-powerful love and how it can guide our lives.

I then focus on the ways we can lose love and how we can begin to get radically honest with ourselves and begin to repair and restore love.

I would firstly like to include an Acronym of Love to help us remember the main points:

- Listen to one another
- Observe and overcome
- Value yourself and value others
- Empower yourself and others

I am going to begin by giving you the definition of Love as I see it:

Love is an expression; a feeling of deep affection and a phenomenon that has no limit; it is inherently unconditional.

Love is about building trust, and it brings about hope and positive mental states. It is relational and involves the integration of emotions, actions and attitude. It is shown through our actions towards others.

Love in itself is a language and a life purpose. It's the virtue that is the light for others to see through us.

It is an attribute of God's divine character and grace.

According to Explore Dictionary.com, Love is a profoundly tender, passionate affection for another person; a feeling of warm personal attachment or deep affection as for a parent, child, or friend.

Love encompasses a variety of different emotions, ranging from subtle to intense; the most sublime, to the simplest pleasures, to the deepest interpersonal affection. Most commonly, we know of Love as a feeling of a strong attraction and emotional attachment that represents kindness, compassion, affection and caring actions.

There are different types of Love: the Love of a mother differs from the Love of a spouse. Affection and Love grow in time. Following the first couple of dates, one should know whether or not there's something there.

In the later stages, genuinely happy couples will reminisce about how their Love and affection for one another grew over time. Imperfections are accepted, even embraced. The Love and devotion you feel for the right person overcomes everything else.

You laugh together a lot. If your relationship lacks humour and laughter, that's usually not a good sign. A mutual sense of humour is among the most essential elements of chemistry.

For those with an astute sense of humour, the right person will probably make you laugh quite often, and vice versa. If not, they may not be the right person. There's a mutual, unshakable sense of respect when it's the right person.

We are not talking about the type of respect shown to one's boss; nor are we talking about morality-based respect. When you've found the right one, the Love and adoration you have for them will be so entrenched that the last thing you'll ever want to do is hurt them.

Both people deeply recognise, appreciate, enjoy, defer and honour each other out of Love and nothing else.

With the right person, your priorities will change. That's what the right person does. You grab each other's hearts, and you both fall in deep love.

For both of you, the period of single life that you enjoyed quickly fades from memory. Not only does it dissolve into the background, but you're thankful that it has because you both want the same things in life and have found the companion for that journey.

This last point is important. Many relationships that end do so because one wants something the other doesn't.

For example, kids, a house, living in a different country, working full-time or staying home, etc. While you won't necessarily want everything the other does, life-changing wants and needs should be mutually agreed upon.

THE PRINCIPLES OF LOVE: THE PATH TO A MORE EXCELLENT WAY OF LIFE

"For God so loved the world that he gave his only begotten son, that whosoever believe in him will not perish but have eternal life." John 3.16.

The following is an exposition of God's Love from the Bible, 1 Corinthians 13:

"Love always protects (defends, guards, shields). Love protects the relationship with loved ones. Love protects and shields loved ones from harm or hurt. Love also protects loved ones from self-harm through a correction in Love. Love defends loved ones regardless of whether they are present or not.

Love always trusts (is convinced). Love trusts and believes in a future that is good for one's self and for the loved ones. Love trusts the loved ones despite present unsteady conditions and is convinced of a better future for the loved ones.

Love is always hopeful (confident, expectant). Love confidently expects things to turn out good for both self and for the beloved.

Love always preserves. Love perseveres for the beloved (persists, continues, sticks with, endures), and continues to remain in expectation of the good while enduring the pain of the moment.

Love encompasses patience and serenity and is kind and thoughtful; it is not jealous or envious.

Love does not brag and is not proud or arrogant.

Love is not rude; it is not self-seeking; it is not easily provoked (nor overly sensitive and easily angered).

Love does not keep score of the wrongs and sins of others.

Love never gives up. Love cares more for others than for self. Love doesn't want what it doesn't have. Instead, it takes pleasure in the flowering of truth.

Love encourages us to trust God always and to never look back.

Love never dies. Inspired speech will be over some day; praying in tongues will end; understanding will reach its limit. We know only a portion of the truth, and what we say about God is always incomplete. But when the Complete arrives, our incomplete will be cancelled.

> *"All friendly feelings for others are an extension of a man's feelings for himself."*
> *Said by Aristotle.*

THE EIGHT DIFFERENT TYPES OF LOVE

"All friendly feelings for others are an extension of a man's feelings for himself."
by Aristotle

I am going to describe the myriad ways we can experience the complex facets of Love.

This encompasses what is felt and experienced in:
- the physical body;
- the mind;
- through memories and emotion,
- through our survival instincts and the unconscious part
- of ourselves,
- and through the soul and spirit.

Eros or Erotic Love (Physical Body)
This is the idea of sexual passion and desire. It is a romantic and sexual feeling. When Eros is misguided, abused and indulged in it leads to impulsive acts and broken hearts.

Affection, Love and friendship (Mind)
It is a type of Love that is felt among friends who have endured hard times together.

Storge or Familiar Love (Memories)
Kinship and Familiarity is a natural form of affection that often flows between parents and their children. It's also found among childhood friends that are later shared as adults.

Ludus or Playful Love (Emotion)
This is a playful form of love, e.g., the affection between young lovers. This is the feeling we have when we go through the early stages of falling in love with someone. Playfulness in love is an essential ingredient that can often be lost in long-term relationships. It is a secret to keeping the

childlike innocence of your love alive, and to keep it interesting and exciting.

Mania Obsessive (Survival instinct)
This is when there is an imbalance between Eros and Ludus, and can lead to obsessiveness. A person can become possessive, jealous, desperate and demanding.

Pragma or Enduring Love (Unconsciousness)
Pragma is a love that has aged, matured and developed over many years into a unique harmony. This is where the couple has spent much time together, and they empower one another.

This type of love is not found but developed, and it requires time and energy. Both sides need to sacrifice, endure, tolerate and develop the patience to make the relationship work. This is a love that gives room for learning and improving.

Philautia or Self-love (Soulful)
This is a Love that requires we care for ourselves and prepare ourselves before sharing our Love with someone else. This is the type of love that many of us fail to understand. This Love is healthy and rewarding.

Agape or Selfless Love (Spirit)
This is unconditional Love; spiritual love; a boundless compassionate love that is without desires and expectations, regardless of the flows and shortcomings of others. This Love can be classified as intuition, divine truth; acceptance, forgiveness and belief. The components of this love are genuine intimacy, commitment, compassion and caring.

A NOTE ON GOD'S LOVE

God is love, and those that worship him must worship in spirit and in truth.

God's laws and principles are the embodiment of love, and they require us to love God, ourselves and others. His grace is sufficient for us to keep his laws and principles. It takes determination and discipline and a level of understanding and maturity to demonstrate this kind of love.

SOME ADVICE ON SELF LOVE

Always be you. Never try to hide who you are. The only shame is to have shame.

Always stand up for what you believe in. Question what other people tell you. Never regret the past, it's a waste of time.

There's a reason for everything. Every mistake, every moment of weakness, every terrible thing that has happened to you, you can release and grow through.

The only way you can ever get the respect of others is when you show them that you respect yourself.

You cannot share what you do not have. If you do not love yourself, you cannot love anyone else either. The only way to truly be happy is to find that unconditional love for yourself. Often learning to love yourself involves embracing all the qualities you perceive as "unlovable".

Know who you are, and understand yourself, embrace your imperfection. Know your strength and your weakness, increase your strength to minimise your faults, seek the opportunity around you and be aware of the threats; be calm and focused.

Know your purpose on earth and be passionate about it, recognise your gifts and visualise your intentions and purpose. Be determined, disciplined and diligent in your personal development.

Self-knowledge is the key to all relationships. When you know yourself, you will know who to relate with, see where you are going, and love God with all your soul and spirit.

Develop your value by developing your discipline.
People admire and trust others who are disciplined, and it is the root of good leadership and impactful actions.

Your vision controls your actions and defines what you do.

Look Inside!! We were taught to look outside ourselves for all the things we thought were missing from our lives. The truth is that there is a life-force within each person, and we discover over time that our heart and soul are a lot wiser than we may first think.

We need to get into the habit of conversing with our souls—listening and trusting the one that created us.

We soon discover that all the answers we were once so desperately seeking outside ourselves, are within us when we converse with the creator.

You are more valuable than all the labels that have been placed on you. You are neither a finished product nor a fixed being. Who you are is constantly changing, growing, and developing. You will become new and better every day.

You should not wait for others to validate your self-worth. Other people cannot determine how worthy and valuable you indeed are. Most people have no idea how valuable THEY are.

Most people allow external things, places, people, and circumstances to determine how much they are worth. So they judge you as being worthy or not so worthy, based on the same criteria.

You should know that these things have nothing to do with your value and self-worth. Don't fall into the trap of thinking that who you are is not enough and that you need other people's approval, love, and validation for you to feel worthy or valuable.

Never allow external things, places, people, or circumstances to determine how much you're worth, and there is no need to compare or compete with anyone or anything else. The life you are meant to create and the person you were born to be is unique.

Your path in life is different from everybody else's and this is a thing to be celebrated.

> "Love is one of the most misunderstood elements of life".

I am now going to dive into the main reasons as to why we lose love throughout our lives.

The reasons we lose love:

- Breach of confidence
- Broken trust
- Endless disappointments
- Unbearable competition
- Opinion, comparison and judgement
- Loss of physical attraction
- Merged identity
- Letting yourself go physically or mentally
- Failing to share activities
- Less personal relating
- Harbouring anger
- Mentally drained
- Stuck on the sofa- loss of interest and motivation, signs of depression.
- No company of others - No social life
- Constant bother, provocation, irritating, annoyance.
- Picking fights.
- Intimacy lost, e.g. hugs and kisses are one of the first casualties when someone starts losing interest in their relationship.
- Wandering Eyes for others.
- Non- disclosure - the level of confusion about one another determines the state of maturity.
- Boredom
- Assumptions
- Unmet expectations - We expect our partner to behave or treat us in a certain way.
- Layers of tensions, stress, distorted perceptions and unwanted baggage
- Perceptions of Love

- No time to study our partner's personalities and love language.
- No skills in love giving.

Let us be honest with ourselves.

- Nothing will change until we change.
- We can avoid toxic partnerships, and toxic situations CAN be reduced.
- These are the following points we need to focus on to develop more honesty and begin to tackle these toxic situations in our relationships.
- We need to become aware of the problematic situation, admit to our part in it and seek help.
- We need to start focusing on self-care and self-love and managing our own emotions.
- We need to fully understand and embrace the fact that no one is perfect, and no condition is permanent.
- We need to understand that negative forces are acting upon our lives and to stop blaming and shaming ourselves.
- We need to free ourselves from bitterness and destruction.
- We need to embrace discipline and determination in love.
- We need to appreciate the process that we all individually go through. These have different elements and timings for each person.
- We need to learn to communicate well for better understanding in our relationships.
- We need to move away from nagging and complaining, towards the patience to truly listen and tolerate circumstances as they are.
- We need to disconnect at times from the many issues we have circulating through our heads, to connect better to the present moment and embrace life as it is.
- We need to understand when we are in dangerously abusive situations and get ourselves out before more damage is done
- We need to know when to talk and when to stop talking. We need to understand how to support one another and develop boundaries.
- We must keep in mind that these elements apply to both men and women.

Practical ways to keep the fire of love burning

- We first need to understand what a person likes and wants in love; their love language.
- How do they respond to your way of giving love? What communicates to them more effectively that you love them? Do these things regularly. Little acts daily make a significant difference.
- Let honour, praise, admiration, appreciation and respect be central pillars in your lives. Let yourself settle into your roles and find balance.
- Be warm towards them, and act intimately, embrace them, comfort them. Let your partner know you love them and how blessed you are to have them.
- Do things that make you both feel proud and progress as a couple. Surprise them!
- Honour each other's family and friends.
- Remember, be quick to say, "I'm sorry dear," and be ready and quick to forgive.
- Always pray for them and pray together often.

The Love We Lost

MICRO JOURNAL

Dates	

MICRO JOURNAL

Dates	

CHAPTER 3

Q & A OF LOVE AND RELATIONSHIP

"The quality of a man is in the state of his mind; you will only attract what you believe and think about, knowledge is required to empower you. The worst retirement is the retirement of the mind!"
Elizabeth Lucas-Afolalu

We have to make various decisions throughout our lives when it comes to love. We may have many questions that we need answers to, to ensure we have a long-lasting enriching relationship. Instead of writing principles, this chapter is in a question and answer format. I believe that I have answered the main questions that would arise in regards to our loving relationships.

The following questions are on the subjects of communication, trust, compatibilities, insecurities, priorities, intimacy, and challenging life events.

How often do you communicate together and understand what is being said?

At the start of the relationship, conversations are exciting and fun. Both of you spend a lot of time getting to know each other. But as time goes by, lovers may forget to ask the same questions again. We're all changing all the time, in our preferences and the way we look at life. Don't assume you know everything about each other. Your romance will start to stagnate, or one of you will begin to confide in some other person who seems more understanding.

How do we communicate effectively?

The rapport between you is essential. Listening and respecting your partner's opinions is paramount.

Correcting their beliefs to incorporate the most loving and respectful viewpoint is valuable. Allowing them to express themselves is a must. It is our responsibility to manage our emotions and our tones of voice, (how we come across to the other person) We must show we love and want to inspire them through our conversations daily, and we must build them up regularly.

Do you trust your partner? There are two kinds of trust in a relationship. Firstly, do you trust your partner enough to feel comfortable with them going out for dinner with someone else? If you don't, perhaps, you're insecure, or your relationship is still too fragile. And secondly, do you trust your partner's decisions? Do you think your partner is capable of making important decisions for both of you? If you can't trust your partner with life-altering decisions, it's evident that you may not respect your partner or their opinions. And that's never a good sign in a long-term relationship. More effective communication needs to be established to figure these big questions out.

How do I handle jealousy and insecurity?

Insecure couples are forever locked in a cycle of jealousy and anger. When you feel jealous about the attention your lover's getting or their recent promotion, you're not helping them become a better individual. It's like a parent who's angry with their child because the child is having "too much fun". You need to learn to have faith in each other and the relationship. Instead of letting negativity build, learn to enjoy each other's successes. After all, your partner is your other half. Any accomplishments of theirs are your accomplishments too, don't you think?

Are we compatible?

Love at first sight and infatuation can last several months. And it does a good job of masking any differences in a relationship. As perfect as two people may be, sometimes, they may just not be ideal for each other.

Love and relationships are like building a house, it's an investment, and it takes patience for you to see the interest, the benefits and enjoy the fruits of your labour together. It takes time, and it might be too early to claim that you are not compatible.

How willing are you in building this love and understanding it better? If you find yourself dating someone with whom you have nothing in common, you need to decide on the next step. Try to find common interests that both of you like, or walk separate paths instead of living in frustrations, and disappointments.

I have a loss of sex drive, what can I do in this situation?

Over time, both of you are bound to lose the sexual urge of the first few months or years of a relationship. While both of you may have a hard time keeping your hands off each other to begin with, now sex may start to feel like a chore.

There may be many reasons, and you should try to find out the issues that are affecting both of you, such as health issues, stress and worries, busyness, etc.

These issues are very common in relationships, and yet, they can be quite simple to solve.

Always look for new ways to recreate the sexual high of the first few times.

What do you do when your spouse's sex life has been challenged due to health issues or some occurring situation?

When the sexual excitement and enthusiasm fade away, what do you have to hold both of you together? A relationship should never be based on sex alone. It needs compatibility and understanding, and it needs dependability.

Staying in love forever is not easy, but with a little effort, it can give meaning to your life. Common reasons for sexual difficulties include traumatic sexual experiences, poor communication, stress, depression, other medical complications like medicines causing a low sex drive, negative experiences causing temporary problems, lack of sexual knowledge, and general disharmony in the relationship.

My advice would be to seek professional help to work through and manage these issues, and talk about it with your partner, humbly, openly and honestly.

What can you say about possessions and materialism?

Anyone in a relationship for long enough will know just how important money or the lack of it really is.

If your friends earn a lot more than you or your partner, it'll end up frustrating both of you.

It will take gratitude, proper money management, and wisdom to build upon your current lives if that is what you want. If you cannot or do not want to for whatever reason, acceptance and gratitude of your situation are key.

It's a stupid fact of life, but our happiness is extremely dependent on the way others perceive us. If you're having difficulties in your relationship because of money, perhaps you could branch out to meet people in a more similar position, and see the difference that makes in your lives.

What can you say about changes in priorities?

You may be in a relationship and in love, but that doesn't change who you are. And that's where the problem starts. As individuals, we evolve all the time. You're not the person you were last year, and you won't be the person you are now next year. And just like you, your partner is also changing constantly.

Now and then, you and your partner may experience changes that will pull both of you apart from each other. And soon enough, both of you may have nothing in common. Spend enough time with each other and try to evolve together in a similar direction.

Talk about your beliefs and your interests with each other. It will help both of you grow together along the same path.

Find a way to express different opinions respectfully in the right moments.

Focus on changing yourself rather than changing your partner as that is impossible. Maybe the positive changes you create in your own life will have a great impact on the relationship.

How often should we spend time together? Do both of you have enough time to spend with each other? These days, time is a luxury that many lovers can't afford. When you start spending too much time away from each other, it's only a matter of time before one of you starts asking the big question;

Do I need my partner in my life anymore?

 Don't drift away so far that both of you don't need to be with each other anymore. Find ways to indulge in exciting hobbies or spend evenings going out on little coffee or ice cream dates or do exercise together like walking. Regularly taking part in activities together will bring you closer and give you more to talk about.

What about giving space and individual growth?

 Now, this is contradictory to the earlier problem in relationships, but it's still something to watch out for. Too much of a good thing can turn out to be bad as well.

When you're in a relationship, spending time with each other is very important. But at the same time, spending time away from each other is crucial too. By spending too much time together, you'd subconsciously feel isolated from the rest of the world. And when that happens, you'd crave for any attention from other interesting people just to feel better about yourself and your ability to communicate. And you know what could happen when that happens, right? It could lead you down a path of dissatisfaction because you have not invested in the right balance.

By the way, are you still in love?

Great question, this is the biggest problem in a relationship and one that's the hardest to overcome. Falling in love is easy. Staying in love isn't. Love is a delicate balance between dependency and passion. How much do you need your partner? How much do you love and want your partner?

How Can I stay in love forever?

Learn – In order for you to learn, listen carefully and observe. Observe the other persons body language. Clarify information and also look towards the most empathetic approach. Keep your heart open at all times.

How do you feel when you meet a long lost love? Emotional memories from the past, including lost love memories, are stored in a primitive area of the brain as feelings and cannot be forgotten. The best thing to do is accept they are there.

Do rekindled lovers learn from the mistakes they made last time?

It is necessary to clear the air about what went wrong first time around and ask for forgiveness.

What would you do when love was interrupted and time wasn't given for it to mature and work out?

1. Recognise and admit that there is a problem that needs addressing.
2. Seek help quickly in the right place and from the right people e.g.
- Professional counselling
- Pastoral counselling
- Elder's Wisdom
3. Pray until something happens (PUSH); pray together always
4. Get support from others but watch who you share your problems with and avoid bad influences.
5. Break down generational curses, chains and barriers, trace the root of the problem and tackle it and get delivered.
6. Once the problem is solved, be willing to share the testimony and help others that are facing the same challenges.

7. Believe "with God all things are possible, and there is nothing too difficult for God to do".

8. If you have resentment against someone else, use this time to forgive him or her. Things don't go as planned. Learn to forgive and forgive quickly. It will reflect in your emotions, and it will lead to peace and joy

9. Hebrews 12:14-15 warns, "Make every effort to live in peace with everyone and to be holy; without holiness, no one will see the Lord. See to it that no one falls short of the grace of God and that no bitter root rises to cause trouble and defile many."

10. It takes patience, tolerance, wisdom and grace of God to build and maintain a relationship.

How do you deal with people's wrong perceptions of you?

People may have their opinion about you, but you don't have to listen. People can emulate or pull you down, but you don't have to allow them to; just ignore them and move forward. Be secure about who you are, and stay focused on where you are going and what you want to become. Be aware of where your values lie and raise your standards to match your values.

What is the best way to overcome "flesh and lust"?

Trust God to help you and pray about the issue. You have to remember your goals and intentions (why you are staying faithful).

Determine to be committed to your love and talk about it with your spouse. Be vulnerable, open and honest.

Determination, discipline and prayer work!

Removing yourself and not putting yourself into situations that would lead to unfavourable outcomes is essential.

There are many benefits of overcoming flesh and lust. It protects you, your spouse and your children; and most importantly, it protects your future and the future of your family.

Do you care to study your partner?

Approach this with a humble heart and a humble spirit.
Cut off all feelings of entitlement. Aim to serve your spouse and be appreciative.
Always remind yourself that love brings reassurance, security and support.
Ask them questions! Watch what makes them happy and record their challenges
and triumphs.
Ask yourself: Are we making any sacrifices toward our love?
Am I willing to go the extra mile for the one I love?

How can I manage conflicts? -

We have to keep in mind that cooperative and constructive communication is key. We are all individuals with different backgrounds, behaviours, perceptions, thoughts, beliefs; and we have different ways of displaying love and affection.
These are things to talk about in your relationship.

LOVE ACRONYM: Listen, Overcome, Value, Enjoy.
- Recognition
- Commitment
- Awareness
- Nourishment
- Learning from storms
- Overcoming issues
- Valuing
- SWOT
- Forgiveness
- Enjoying life

Should your partner bring their past into their current situations?

It depends on how much progress they have made in learning from their mistakes. It also depends if they have forgiven themselves and the other person.

How does the situation affect their mental state today?

Couples must be open and understanding when talking about these things; reserving judgment, jealousy and negativity: talking to truly understand. Then a way for you to support your partner will surface, and you can help them progress past their current state.

Heartbreaks are our greatest teachers. Give the person time and space to heal from their issues. Extend them grace.

How do I deal with my partner's past?

There is a reason the past is in the past. Normalise both your feelings and validate the pain you both feel. The past is no longer 'real'. Let go of past relationships because you do not want to protect it onto your current one.

Our memories and experiences from our last relationship can come back to haunt us.

If forgetting and managing these memories and feelings is a challenge, I suggest seeking counsel and pray about it.

Can you fall back in love with someone who hurt you?

Beauty can be found in forgiveness and diligence.
A person accepting responsibility and asking for forgiveness is the start. But it is not straightforward. More counsel should be sort on an ongoing basis to deal with the feelings and issues that surface through the process of repair and forgiveness.

Both of you can learn much about the process of forgiveness.
Appreciating the present moment, being honest with feelings and talking through things is key.

God forgave us; we should extend this grace and mercy to others.
As mentioned before, forgiveness does not mean you forget, and sometimes relationships have to stay severed despite forgiveness; you know in your heart. You can reconnect if you reevaluate the situation and also keep in mind what severed you in the first place. Reaching a shared understanding is crucial. Reassess how problems are triggered and work towards healing and managing those triggers.

Why is it so essential to reunite and reconnect?

It can be a great choice to reunite with your love again if you have lost the initial relationship. Everyone makes mistakes, but there are so many ways we can learn from them. It will allow you to develop better understanding and patience, and appreciation for the fallibility of human nature. It feels good to try hard at repairing something; the sense of accomplishment in progress can be incredible. Your honesty and renewed trust, resulting in harmony and peace, can influence others and restore hope and faith. It ultimately promotes humanity and community.

How can the couple overcome their feeling of being overwhelmed?

Accepting and communicating that one is overwhelmed is the crucial first step.

Couples that pray together are more likely to stay together!
Positivity and hope that things will get better is a must.
Both partners should be active together, share responsibilities and have fun together.
Scheduled relaxation time is key.

Progress, not perfection! You dont have to solve all your problems at once, but an attitude of kindness and patience will allow you the time to endure the challenges you face.
Sometimes alone time can work!

How can we prevent arguing so much?

Give your partner plenty of time to express themselves without cutting them off. Getting to know the fullness of how they think and feel is an essential part of connecting genuinely and finding common ground through any challenges. If you keep pushing your thoughts and feelings over listening to theirs, this is where relationship problems get free rein. Interrupting your partner leads to arguments.

Listen to their position and seek to recognise and understand what underlying emotional needs that haven't been met and how you can restore that. Ask questions in a neutral tone of voice and avoid making assumptions.If you are reluctant to listen to them; remember that listening does not imply that you are agreeing. Repeat what you think you have heard in your own words; summarise to check that you have understood as much as possible, brainstorm for solutions together.

I am now going to mention some important points about identifying abuse and getting the correct support in place.

How do I know if I am experiencing abuse?

If you answer yes to one or more of the following questions, you may be in an abusive relationship.

- Has your partner tried to keep you from seeing your friends or family?
- Has your partner prevented you from continuing or starting or continuing education, or from going to work?
- Does your partner constantly check up on you or follow you?
- Does your partner accuse you unjustly of flirting or of having affairs?
- Does your partner constantly belittle or humiliate you, or regularly criticise or insult you in front of other people?
- Are you ever scared of your partner?
- Have you ever changed your behaviour because you're afraid of what your partner might do or say to you?
- Has your partner ever deliberately destroyed any of your possessions?
- Has your partner ever hurt or threatened you?
- Has your partner ever kept you short of money, so you're unable to buy food and other necessary items for yourself?
- Has your partner ever forced you to do something that you didn't want to do, including sexually?

If you think you may be in an abusive relationship, there are lots of people who can help you. There are some necessary steps you can take to support anyone who confides in you that they're suffering domestic abuse:

- Listen to them and take care not to blame them. Tell the person that there are many people in the same situation of relationship abuse.
- Acknowledge that it takes strength to talk to someone about experiencing abuse.
- Give the person time to talk, but don't push the person to speak if they don't want to.
- Acknowledge that the person is in a frightening and challenging situation.
- Tell the person that no one deserves to be threatened or beaten, despite what their abuser has told them. Nothing they do or say justifies the abuser's behaviour.
- Support the person as a friend. Encourage the person to express their feelings and allow them to make their own decisions.
- Don't tell them to leave the relationship if they aren't ready. That's their decision.
- Ask if the person has suffered physical harm. If so, offer to go with them to a hospital or GP.
- Help them to report the assault to the police if they choose to.
- Be ready to provide information on organisations that offer help.

Domestic violence, also called domestic abuse, includes physical, emotional and sexual abuse in couple relationships or between family members. It's abuse if your partner or a family member: threatens you; shoves or pushes you; makes you fear for your physical safety; puts you down, or attempts to undermine your self-esteem; controls you, for example by stopping you seeing your friends and family; is jealous and possessive, such as being suspicious of your friendships and conversations.

It is essential to seek help before things get worse. Still, it is understandable if a person feels unsure and scared to do so because of the repercussions. There are many ways to overcome this.

MICRO JOURNAL

Dates	

MICRO JOURNAL

Dates	

CHAPTER 4

THE TRUTH ABOUT LOVE

God is love and those that believe him must love others. The underlying principles of his commandments focus on love; loving ourselves, loving God and loving everyone around us.

I am going to include passages from the bible to illuminate what love means for us.

It states in 1 Corinthians 7:1–40

"Nevertheless, because of sexual immorality, let each man have his wife, and let each woman have her husband. Let the husband render to his wife the affection due her, and likewise also the wife to her husband. The wife does not have authority over her own body, but the husband does. And likewise, the husband does not have authority over his own body, but the wife does. Do not deprive one another except with consent for a time, that you may give yourselves to fasting and prayer; and come together again so that Satan does not tempt you because of your lack of self-control. (Read entire text) (NKJV)

Jesus displayed the greatest love in all of human history by literally laying down His life for His friends. That is you and I if we are born again. Jesus died for us while we were his enemies, still sinners, and hostile to the things of God (Rom 5).

You may not have to lay down your life in the sense of dying for others but laying down your life is investing time, talents, and treasure in esteeming others better than yourself (Phil 2:3). Our life consists of only a short time on this earth. So when we lay down our lifetimes in serving others, we are laying down our time for others, and we are no more like God than when we sacrifice what we want for what others need.

Ephesians 4:2-3 "Be completely humble and gentle; be patient, bearing with one another in love. Make every effort to keep the unity of the spirit through the bond of peace." The church must strive for unity and a "bond of peace" and this can only be done when we remain humble, patient and bear "with one another in love." Paul knows this is not easy and why he writes that we must "make every effort to keep the unity of the Spirit." Relationships take work. Everyone has different preferences, so we must have love in accepting one another's differences. God accepted us through Christ when we didn't deserve it.

John 3:16 For God so loved the world that he gave his only begotten son, that whosoever believe in him shall not perish but have eternal life.

John 15:16 "Greater love has no one than this; that he lay down his life for his friends."

Jesus displayed the greatest love in all of human history by literally laying down His life for His friends. That is you and I if we are born again. Jesus died for us while we were his enemies, still sinners, and hostile to the things of God (Rom 5). You may not have to lay down your life in the sense of dying for others but laying down your life is investing time, talents, and treasure in esteeming others better than yourself (Phil 2:3).

Our life consists of only a short time on this earth, and so when we lay down our lifetimes in serving others, we are laying down our time for others, and we are no more like God than when we sacrifice what we want for what others need.

Corinthians 13:1 If I speak in the tongues of men and angels, but have not love, I am a noisy gong or a clanging cymbal. And if I have prophetic powers, and understand all mysteries and all knowledge. If I have all faith to remove mountains but have not love, I am nothing. If I give away all I have, and if I deliver up my body to be burned, but have not love, I gain nothing.

Colossians 3:18-19 "Wives, be in subjection to your husbands, as is fitting in the Lord. Husbands, love your wives, and be not bitter against them."

Ephesian 5:22-25 "Wives, be in subjection unto your own husbands, as unto the Lord. For the husband is the head of the wife, as Christ also is the head of the church, being himself the saviour of the body. But as the church is subject to Christ, so let the wives also be to their husbands in everything. Husbands, love your wives, even as Christ also loved the church, and gave himself up for it"

Facts about Married Couples

The fear of God is the beginning of wisdom, and marriages are blessed and ordained by the holy institution.

A virtuous woman builds her home with this wisdom. The man will also be affected by the fear of God.

The relationship with God directly reflects the relationship between two people in marriage, and it is about obeying the principles laid out by him, and seeking help where necessary.

He regularly mentions that love is about patience, understanding and endurance; tolerance and seeking prayer together.

He states that love is not about pride, competition, arrogance, violence, pretence, deceit, nor suffering silently.

We all need one another; The Male is for strength while the Female is for comfort; the supporter and home builder. Man needs influence and woman was called to fill a need and a gap. The woman is not in competition with a man; "Those who know the situation, correct the situation and those who understand their assignment, focus on their assignment and be fulfilled; be one of them."

Women are chosen to solve emotional problems and to be the connector between God and man. They are designed to stay in God's presence to hear God for their husbands and to be filled with joy and peace.

A woman needs to be nourished for the man, for their glory and beauty to radiate. Creation got involved because a woman stepped in. Women were called to fulfil their purpose, which is to be mothers of families; mothers of communities, and mothers of nations and generations.

Women were called to take God's nourishment to strengthen them, and to go deep into a relationship with him. Their connection with the universe will help them joyfully build and support their husbands.

God is their helper, supporter, and strength. A woman's potential and wisdom dictates and produces nourishment.

Sight is the limitation of man, but vision is the prerequisite of the Highest God. We must work not by sight, nor by fear, arrogance, pride, jealousy, envy, nor by power, might, competition, copying, condemning, judging nor race, but by the spirit of God in us.

Man was called and ordained to be leaders, protectors, providers and priests. He who finds A WIFE finds A GOOD THING and obtains FAVOUR from GOD.

A wife is a precious thing to look for and find, and man is blessed because of this. A man upon finding a wife, leaves his family to take full responsibility for this precious diamond, to obtain favour from God.

A husband should love and cherish his wife, and the wife should respect and submit to her husband.

The favour they cultivate between them expands and multiplies to obtain the blessing of children.

Children are the heritage of God, and Children are for signs and wonders. Children are generational seeds from God.

To conclude the matter in this chapter; we crave to feel connected and to be in relationships from the second we are born. We need to feel love and acceptance. The first relationships we have are with our parents. We look to them to nurture us. We learn so much from them – good and bad; depending upon their beliefs and morals. As we grow older, we develop friendships – both platonic and romantic. Many of us become parents ourselves. We continue to learn from every person we develop a relationship with.

And then there are acquaintances – people we know. We might hang out with them some times, but their lives don't particularly intertwine with ours. They're usually not our first choice to go to dinner with. Their life struggles do not personally affect us in any way. We learn to share. We learn teamwork. We develop likes and dislikes. We tend to gravitate towards people we look up to, and this could also be people we fear. I always told my kids, "Be careful of who you hang out with because you will develop some of their traits." It's just human nature. I think that's one of the reasons why it's so easy for couples to finish each other's sentences—the more time you spend with someone, the more like them you become.

I believe that the relationships we have with others determine our real character. Family and friends will be there in our times of struggle – strangers and acquaintances will scarcely be seen. In the movie "It's a Wonderful Life" Clarence the Angel writes, "Remember, George: no man is a failure who has friends." With friends and people by our side, we can accomplish anything. We must build strong relationships with those we love. They are the ones that matter the most to us. We should always treat them as such. Never take them for granted. Value the unique aspect of each individual. Can you imagine how boring life would be if we were all the same? Treat everybody with respect. Accept people where they are. Allow them to make their own choices in life. Remember you can't change anyone but yourself. Concentrate on being the best person and the best friend you can be – and you'll have no problem establishing and retaining real, long-lasting relationships.

An essential factor of ensuring that love is protected and maintained in a relationship is by helping and supporting your partner to cope with life's challenges.

What you can do to help your partner cope with stress.

- Encourage them to look for ways to deal with the daily stressors in life
- Act as a sounding board and refrain from making judgments
- Give advice only when asked
- Give them some extra positive attention
- Soothe them through hard times
- Ask them what they need

Stress, whether from inside or outside of a relationship, is likely to affect the way you think, feel and behave; and will invariably impact your partner.

Relationship stress can be caused by:

- Never-ending criticism;
- Feeling unheard;
- Disagreements over chores;
- Sexual problems;
- Work-related problems;
- Financial difficulties;
- Arguments etc.
- As a result of a crisis
- sudden illness,
- the death of a loved one

Avoiding issues can provide temporary relief, but these factors take a toll over time. They can reduce a person's resilience when confronted with further stressful situations. I'm sure you're aware that there are physical consequences too - the impact of stress can make you ill

10 Things you can do to deal with relationship stress effectively.

1. Calm yourself or do whatever you can to calm your partner - as human beings we're much better at finding solutions when we're calm.
2. Accept that your partner can't read your mind. Reading someone's face can be unreliable.
3. Understand that your partner is going to react, deal with stress and solve problems differently than you would, you may not like or understand their ways!
4. Realise that your and your partner's time scale may be very different!
5. Write down your thoughts - it will help you to be more objective. Have a look at my journaling page for further information.
6. Address any external sources of stress.
7. State clearly if something is entirely unacceptable to you.

8. Take care of yourself. Get enough sleep, eating well and exercising regularly.
9. Engage in meaningful and enjoyable activities, even if it seems too much of an effort to start with.
10. Consider taking some gentle natural remedies.

10 Occasions when it's not a good time to have a major discussion

1. When one or both of you are under the influence of alcohol - an absolute 'no, no'.
2. When one or both of you are about to go out.
3. When you're driving.
4. When there are other people around.
5. When your children can overhear (though they need not be protected from well-debated disagreements)
6. When you're tired, hungry or ill.
7. When you feel particularly stressed.
8. When it's a 'special' days (birthdays, Christmas, etc.) - the memory of a negative event is likely to hang around much longer.
9. When you already know that there is a better time!
10. When you've had little sleep.

Nature requires one to escape anything that looks or feels like it's limiting us; obligations and expectations. Love needs space to grow and needs a little breathing room; love dies under heavy limitations because we cannot help but expand, help but evolve and help but change. So when limitation occurs, there is a tendency that we want to break out of them by breaking up, we expect specific behaviour. We hurt others and ourselves because of fear; we are scared that love cannot be boxed in, be dictated or forced or obligated. If love is going to grow or flourish, it has to be free.

MICRO JOURNAL

Dates	

MICRO JOURNAL

Dates	

CHAPTER 5

FORGIVENESS

Someone that can never forgive is someone destined to be alone. Forgiveness is one of the ways you can profoundly change your life. It's not always easy, but it's a skill that can be learned. It just takes practice. Forgiving and forgetting is a skill that requires work to become good at. But be smart. If someone took advantage of you at work, it doesn't mean you shouldn't be careful to prevent it from happening again. Forgiving means that you should let it go, so you don't have to be miserable thinking about that person every day for years to come.

Forgiving others is essential for spiritual growth. Your experience of someone who has hurt you, while painful, is now nothing more than a thought or feeling that you carry around. These thoughts of resentment, anger, and hatred represent slow, debilitating energies that will disempower you if you continue to let these thoughts occupy space in your head. If you could release them, you would know more peace.

NEGATIVE EXPERIENCES, EMOTIONAL WOUNDS AND FORGIVENESS - Negative experiences and emotional wounds can leave you with lasting feelings of anger, bitterness, or even vengeance. But if you don't practice forgiveness, you might be the one who pays most dearly, as the cycle of pain, hurt, and unforgiveness continue. By embracing forgiveness, you can also embrace peace, hope, gratitude, and joy. Forgiveness can lead you to physical, emotional, and spiritual healing and well-being.

Turn your hurts over to God, and allow the Spirit to flow through you. Reconnect to Spirit—make a new agreement with yourself to always stay connected to Spirit, even when it seems to be the most challenging thing to do. Your new agreement with reality, in which you've blended your physical self and your personality with your spiritual God-connected self, will begin to radiate a higher energy of love and light. Wherever you go, others will experience the glow of your God-consciousness, and disharmony and disorder and all manner of problems simply will not flourish in your presence. Become "an instrument of thy peace," as St. Francis desires in the first line of his famous prayer.

Negative emotions are tools that can tell us that something might be wrong. For your best results, take the appropriate action at the time something happens, and then be done with the emotion. Forgive and move on with your life! Nearly everyone has been hurt by the actions or words of another. Perhaps your mother criticised your parenting skills, or your work colleague sabotaged a project etc.

Generally, forgiveness is a decision to let go of resentment and thoughts of revenge. The act that hurt or offended you might always remain a part of your life, but forgiveness can lessen its grip on you and help you focus on other, more positive parts of your life. Forgiveness can even lead to feelings of understanding, empathy, and compassion for the one who hurt you.

What Are the Benefits of Forgiving Someone? Letting go of grudges and bitterness can make way for happiness, health, and peace. Forgiveness can lead to healthier relationships, greater spiritual and psychological well-being, less anxiety, less stress and hostility, lower blood pressure, fewer symptoms of depression, a healthier immune system, improved heart health, and higher self-esteem.

Why Is It So Easy to Hold a Grudge? When someone you love and trust hurts you, you might become angry, sad, or confused. If you dwell on hurtful events or situations, grudges filled with resentment, vengeance, and hostility can take root. If you allow negative feelings to crowd out positive feelings, you might find yourself swallowed up by your bitterness or sense of injustice.

What Are the Effects of Holding a Grudge? If you're unforgiving, you might bring anger and bitterness into every relationship, and new experiences.

You might become so wrapped up in the wrong that you can't enjoy the present; you might become depressed or anxious and feel that your life lacks meaning or purpose. You may think that you're at odds with your spiritual beliefs; you might lose valuable and enriching connectedness with others.

A LESSON IN UNFORGIVENESS

This next piece of writing is a story Jesus told in the Bible. Once upon a time, there was a king who wished to settle accounts with his servants. When he began the accounting, one who owed him 10,000 talents was brought to him. However, he could not repay, so his master ordered him to be sold, with his wife and his children and everything that he possessed, and payment to be made. The servant fell on his knees and begged him, saying, "Have patience with me, and I will repay you everything."

And his master's heart was moved with compassion, and he released him and forgave him [cancelling] the debt. However, that same servant went out and found one of his fellow servants who owed him a hundred denarii; and he seized him and began choking him, saying, "Pay what you owe!" So, his fellow servant fell on his knees and begged him, earnestly, "Have patience with me, and I will repay you."

But he was unwilling, and he went and had him thrown in prison until he paid back the debt. When his fellow servants saw what had happened, they were deeply grieved, and they went and reported to their master [with clarity and in detail] everything that had taken place. Then his master called him and said to him, "You wicked and contemptible slave. I forgave all that [great] debt of yours because you begged me. Should you not have had mercy on your fellow slave [who owed you little by comparison], as I had mercy on you?" And in wrath, his master turned him over to the torturers (jailers) until he paid all that he owed. Jesus then said, "My heavenly Father will also do the same to [every one of] you if each of you does not forgive his brother from your heart."

HOW CAN I FORGIVE AND BE FREE?

To begin, consider the value of forgiveness and its importance in your life.

Reflect on the facts of the situation and how it has affected your life, health, and well-being. Forgiveness will help you move away from your role as victim and release the control and power that the offending person and situation have had on your life, and as you let go of grudges, you'll no longer define your life by how you've been hurt.

Unforgiveness is the root of bitterness; it robs us of the full life God intends for us. Rather than promote justice, our forgiveness festers into distress. Hebrews 12:14–15 warns, "Make every effort to live in peace with everyone and to be holy; without holiness, no one will see the Lord. See to it that no one falls short of the grace of God and that no bitter root rises to cause trouble and defile many."

Similarly, 2 Corinthians 2:5–11 warns that forgiveness can be an opening for Satan to derail us. If you have resentment against someone else, use this time to forgive him or her. Learn to forgive and forget quickly. It will reflect in your emotions and give you peace and joy. Identify what happened, identify what it caused you, tell God what happened, and release the hurt caused by the offender to the court of God, which is scary for the offender. Now they have to answer to God, a much Higher Court because forgiveness does not let the offender off the hook! It just releases you from the burden of carrying it, and so it is for your good. Tell the offender you have chosen to forgive—which is the process of releasing the matter to God's jurisdiction.

Forgiving someone does not mean the offence or hurt didn't happen. Forgiveness doesn't necessarily resume trust. I know through experience that when we choose to forgive and allow that to work within our hearts, doing away with anger, hurt, bitterness, fear, thoughts of self-pity or self-righteousness, then the event becomes nothing but a memory. We can bless those who have injured us, with a sincere heart, and we may even be willing to return to the relationship if it is safe to do so. This way, if it is a relationship that God needs for us to get back into, we can build again what God intended to build the first time before the offence happened.

 Some of your healing and miracles require your forgiveness to yourself and others. Let the offence go, and let your miracle come in. Forgiveness enables you to turn your back to bitterness. If you have a regret about something you've done, use this moment to forgive yourself. If you have resentment against someone else, use this time to forgive them. Forgiveness is a commitment to a process of change. The remaining sections of this chapter are devoted to helping you to understand how to stay in a state of forgiveness.

DOES FORGIVENESS GUARANTEE RECONCILIATION? If the hurtful event involved someone whose relationship you otherwise value, forgiveness can lead to reconciliation. However, this isn't always the case. An agreement might be impossible if the offender has died or is unwilling to communicate with you. In other cases, reconciliation might not be appropriate. Still, forgiveness is possible—even if reconciliation isn't.

Having to interact with the person who hurt you may be difficult. If you haven't reached a state of forgiveness, being near the person who hurt you might prompt you to be tense and stressful. To handle these situations, remember that you can choose to attend or avoid specific functions and gatherings.

If you choose to attend, don't be surprised by a certain amount of awkwardness and perhaps even more intense feelings. Respect yourself and do what seems best, doing your best to keep an open mind. You might find that the experience helps you to move forward with forgiveness.

WHEN IT'S YOU WHO NEEDS FORGIVENESS? The first step is to honestly assess and acknowledge the wrongs you've done and how those wrongs have affected others. At the same time, avoid judging yourself too harshly. You're human, and you'll make mistakes. If you're genuinely sorry for something you've said or done, consider admitting it to those you've harmed.

Speak of your sincere sorrow or regret, and specifically ask for forgiveness, without making excuses. Remember, however; you can't force someone to forgive you. Others need to move to forgiveness in their own time. Whatever the outcome, commit to treating others with compassion, empathy, and respect.

Step 1: Move On to the Next Act - Recognise your hurts are in the past. It is important to realise that we can let go of the hurts merely by dropping the distressing thoughts and turning towards our feelings to offer them compassion and acceptance.

Step 2: Don't Go to Sleep Angry

In sleep, man impresses the subconscious mind with his conception of himself. — Neville Goddard

Speak these words to yourself at night,

"Each night, as I drift off to sleep, I adamantly refuse to use this precious time to review anything that I do not want to be reinforced in my subconscious mind. I choose to impress upon my subconscious my conception of myself as a Divine creator in alignment with the one mind. My last waking concept of myself will dominate my slumber. I am peaceful, I am content, I am love, and I attract only to myself those who are in alignment with my highest ideals of myself. I eschew any temptation to go over any fear or unpleasantness that my ego might be asking me to review. I assume the feeling in my body of those "I am" statements already fulfilled, and I know that I'm allowing myself to be programmed while asleep, for the next day I rise knowing that I am a free agent.

Step 3: Switch the Focus from Blaming Others; to Understanding Yourself

Whenever you're upset over the conduct of others, take the focus off those you're holding responsible for your inner distress. Shift your mental energy to allowing yourself to be with whatever you're feeling — let the experience be as it may, without blaming others for your feelings. Don't blame yourself either! Just allow the experience to unfold and tell yourself that no one has the power to make you uneasy without your consent and that you're unwilling to grant that authority to this person right now. Tell yourself that you are willing to freely experience your emotions without calling them "wrong" or needing to chase them away. In this way, you've made a shift to self-mastery. It's important to bypass blame, and even to bypass your desire to understand the other person; instead, focus on understanding yourself.

By taking responsibility for how you choose to respond to anything or anyone, you're aligning yourself with life. By changing the way you choose to perceive the power that others have over you, you will see a bright new world of unlimited potential for yourself, and you will know how to forgive and let go of anything instantly.

Step 4: Avoid Telling People What to Do - Avoid thoughts and activities that involve telling people who are perfectly capable of making their own choices what to do. In your family, remember that you do not own anyone.

The poet Kahlil Gibran reminds you: Your children are not your children. They are the sons and daughters of life's longing for itself. They come through you but not from you"

Disregard any inclination to dominate in all of your relationships. Listen rather than dictate. Pay attention to yourself when you're having judgmental opinions and see where self-attention takes you. When you replace an ownership mentality with one of allowing, you'll begin to see how you can effortlessly flow with life.

From that moment on, you'll be free of frustration with those who don't behave according to your ego-dominated expectations.

Step 5: Learn to Let Go and Be Like Water - Rather than attempting to dominate with your forcefulness, be like water: flow everywhere there's an opening. Soften your hard edges by being more tolerant of contrary opinions. Interfere less, and listen more.

When someone offers you their viewpoint, try responding with: "I've never considered that before—thank you. I'll give it some thought." When you give up interfering and opt instead to stream like water—gently, softly, and unobtrusively— you become forgiveness itself.

Picture yourself as having the same qualities as water. Allow your soft, weak, yielding, fluid self to enter places where you previously were excluded because of your inclination to be solid and hard.

Flow softly into the lives of those with whom you feel conflicted: Picture yourself entering their private inner selves, seeing perhaps for the first time what they're experiencing. Keep this image of yourself as gently coursing water, and watch how your relationships change.

Step 6: Take Responsibility for Your Part -

Removing blame means never assigning responsibility to anyone else for what you're experiencing. It means that you're willing to say, "I may not understand why I feel this way, why I have this illness, why I've been victimised, or why I had this accident, but I'm willing to say without any guilt or resentment that I own it. I live with, and I am responsible for, having it in my life." If you take responsibility for having the experience, then at least you have a chance also to take responsibility for removing it or learning from it.

If you're in some small (perhaps unknown) way responsible for that migraine headache or that depressed feeling, then you can go to work to remove it or discover what its message is for you. If, on the other hand, someone or something else is responsible in your mind, then, of course, you'll have to wait until they change for you to get better. And that is unlikely to occur. So you go home with nothing and are left with nothing when peace is really on the other side of the coin.

Step 7: Let Go of Resentments - What causes annoyance and anger after a dispute?

The generic response would be a laundry list detailing why the other person was wrong. It would conclude with something like, "I have a right to be upset when my [daughter, mother-in-law, ex-husband, boss, or whomever you're thinking of] speaks to me that way!" Resentments don't come from the conduct of the other party in an altercation—no, they survive and thrive because you're unwilling to end that altercation with an offering of kindness, love, and authentic forgiveness. So when all of the yelling, screaming, and threatening words have been expressed, the time for calm has arrived. Remember that no storm lasts forever, and that hidden within are always seeds of tranquillity. There is a time for hostility and a time for peace.

Step 8: Be Kind Instead of Right

There is a Chinese proverb, "If you're going to pursue revenge, you'd better dig two graves", which is saying that your resentments will destroy you. The world is just the way it is. The people who are behaving "badly" in the world are doing what they're supposed to be doing. You can process it in any way that you choose. If you're filled with anger about all of those "problems," you are one more person who contributes to the pollution of anger.

Instead, remember that you do not need to make others wrong or to retaliate when you've been wronged.

Imagine if someone says something to you that you find offensive, and rather than opting for resentment, you learn to depersonalise what you've just heard and respond with kindness. You are willing to freely send the higher, faster energies of love, peace, joy, forgiveness, and compassion as your response to whatever comes your way. You do this for yourself. You would rather be kind than right.

Step 9: Practice Giving - In the midst of arguments or disagreements, practice giving rather than taking before you exit. Giving involves leaving the ego behind. While it wants to win and show its superiority by being contrary and disrespectful, your Tao nature wants to be at peace and live in harmony. You can reduce your quarrelling time to almost zero if you practice this procedure: Wherever you are, whenever you feel strong emotions stirring in you and you notice yourself feeling the need to "be right," silently recite the following words from the Prayer of Saint Francis: Where there is injury, [let me bring] pardon. Be a giver of forgiveness as he teaches: Bring love to hate, light to darkness, and pardon to injury.

Read these words daily, for they'll help you overcome your ego's demands and know the fullness of life.

Step 10: Stop Looking for Occasions to Be Offended - When you live at or below ordinary levels of awareness, you spend a great deal of time and energy finding opportunities to be offended. A news report, a rude stranger, someone cursing, a sneeze, a black cloud —just about anything will do if you're looking for an occasion to be offended. Become a person who refuses to be offended by any one, any thing, or any set of circumstances. If you have enough faith in your own beliefs, you'll find that it's impossible to be offended by the beliefs and conduct of others. Not being offended is a way of saying, "I have control over how I'm going to feel, and I choose to feel peaceful regardless of what I observe going on. When you feel offended, you're practicing judgment. You judge someone else to be stupid, insensitive, rude, arrogant, inconsiderate, or foolish, and then you find yourself upset and offended by their conduct. What you may not realise is that when you judge another person, you do not define them. You define yourself as someone who needs to judge others.

Step 11: Don't Live In the Past – Be Present - When we find it difficult to forgive, often it is because we are not living in the present, and instead, we assign more importance to the past. We assign a good portion of our energy and attention lamenting the good old days that are gone forever as the reason why we can't be happy and fulfilled today. "Everything has changed," "No one respects anyone else like they used to..." This is assigning responsibility to the past for why you can't be happy today. It's doubtful that other creatures waste the present moment in thoughts of past and future. A beaver only does beaver, and he does it right in the moment. He doesn't spend his days ruminating over the fact that his beaver siblings received more attention, or his father beaver ran off with a younger beaver when he was growing up. He's always in the now. We can learn much from God's creatures about enjoying the present moment rather than using it up consumed with anger over the past or worry about the future and practice living in the moment by appreciating the beauty around you now.

Step 12: Embrace Your Dark Times - In a universe that's an intelligent system with a divine creative force supporting it, there simply can be no accidents. As tough as it is to acknowledge, you had to go through what you went through in order to get to where you are today, and the evidence is that you did. Every spiritual advance that you will make in your life will very likely be preceded by some kind of fall or seeming disaster. Those dark times, accidents, tough episodes, break ups, periods of impoverishment, illnesses, abuses, and broken dreams were all in order. They happened, so you can assume they had to and you can't unhappy them. Embrace them from that perspective, and then understand them, accept them, honour them, and finally transform them.

Step 13: Refrain from Judgement -

When you stop judging and simply become an observer, you will know inner peace. With that sense of inner peace, you'll find yourself happier and free of the negative energy of resentment. A bonus is that you'll find that others are much more attracted to you. A peaceful person attracts peaceful energy. If I'm to be a being of love living from my highest self, that means that love is all I have inside of me and all that I have to give away. If someone I love chooses to be something other than what my ego would prefer, I must send them the ingredients of my highest self, which is God, and God is love.

My criticism and condemnation of the thoughts, feelings, and behaviour of others—regardless of how right and moral my human self convinces me it is—is a step away from God-realization. And it is God-consciousness that allows for my wishes to be fulfilled, as long as they are aligned with my Source of being. I can come up with a long list of reasons why I should be judgmental and condemnatory toward another of God's children and why

I am right. Yet if I want to perfect my world—and I so want to do so—then I must substitute love for these judgments.

Step 15: Send Love - We are all human: you, me, all of us. We do occasionally slip and retreat from our highest self into judgment, criticism, and condemnation, but this is not a rationale for choosing to practice that kind of interaction. I can only tell you that when I finally got it, and I sent only love to another of God's children whom I had been judging and criticising, I got the immediate result of inner contentment. I urge you to send love in place of those judgments and criticisms to others when you feel they impede your joy and happiness, and hold them in that place of love. Notice that if you stay steadfast, when you change the way you look at things, the things you look at change.

The Love We Lost

MICRO JOURNAL

Dates	

MICRO JOURNAL

Dates	

CHAPTER 6

MANAGING EMOTIONS

Emotional responsibility is an essential ingredient for creating a healthy relationship. When people do not take responsibility for their feelings, they tend to try and make others responsible for their happiness. As adults, happiness, emotional safety, and self-esteem also come from how we treat others and ourselves.

Therefore, we should not be abandoning ourselves but, instead, we should love and value ourselves, and ways to do that include praying, confessing, affirmations and meditations.

Affirmations penetrate deep into your subconscious, passively, without you taking conscious action. They imprint a new set of thinking patterns.

They will aid you to become more aware of how they impact your behaviour and enable you to develop healthier means of handling your emotions. These affirmations will activate the parts of your mind responsible for the way you're dealing with your emotions.

You will develop a clear understanding of why you feel the way you do, and the mechanisms activated when emotion gets too loud. You will be able to choose healthier ways of dealing with it and be better able to understand others, and this will bring about significant improvement in your relationships.

You will no longer be controlled by someone's emotional reaction because, by learning to recognise your own emotions and reactions, you will be better equipped to understand others.

By not letting the emotions govern your life, you will understand what having peace of mind means. You will no longer be finding yourself overwhelmed by sadness, stress, or anger—you will learn to observe them neutrally and to let them go without them leaving a significant mark on you.

AFFIRMATIONS FOR EMOTIONS

I am aware of my emotions.
I am alert to the feelings of those around me.
I pick up on mood changes in myself and others.
I can reason with my emotions.
My emotions are under control.
I manage my feelings.
Understanding emotions come easily to me.
I regulate the feelings of my peers.
I respond appropriately to my senses.
I accurately interpret the emotions of others.
I will focus more on my feelings.
I will acknowledge my emotions.
I will react to the emotions of those around me.
I am becoming confident in my emotional perception.
I will intelligently evaluate others' sentiments.
My emotions will be manageable.
My ability to get along with others will improve.
I will assess the emotions of my peers.
I will be able to build stronger relationships with others.
I am naturally attentive to emotions.
Emotional intelligence is second nature to me.

I naturally know my emotional boundaries.
Others see me as emotionally aware.
I am tuned-in to my emotional well-being.

According to Margaret Paul, Ph.D., a relationship expert, best-selling author, and co-creator of the powerful Inner Bonding® self-healing process, states that relationship problems are a by-product of emotional issues and emotional self-abandonment.

Emotional self-abandonment generally occurs in four ways: ignoring your feelings by staying in your head rather than being present in your body; judging yourself; turning to various addictions to avoid your emotions, and making others responsible for your feelings. However, by doing inner work to become an emotionally accountable, kind and loving person with yourself and with others, you can create a healthy, loving relationship. So, therefore, start learning how to love and connect with yourself so that you can connect with others. I suggest reading her book.

Meditation for Loving Kindness

Picture yourself at the termination of a quarrel or major dispute. Rather than reacting with old patterns of residual anger, revenge, and hurt, visualise offering kindness, love, and forgiveness. Do this right now by sending out these "true virtue" thoughts to any resentment you're currently carrying. Make this your standard response to any future altercations: e.g. I will love, no matter what!

Asking God for guidance.

We pray to God to heal emotions and mental breakdowns, physical and spiritual wounds and ask for forgiveness from God.

We pray Psalm 23 will be your prayer, Psalm 121 will be your testimony, and Psalm 91 will be your covering.

In the mighty name of Jesus, we pray for restoration to every broken relationship, and we pray for healing, understanding, patience, trust, love and forgiveness.

We pray at this moment for God to intervene in every situation that is destroying our relationships.

We pray Abba father, to keep the fire of love burning and give them new anointing, new hope, a new beginning, new joy and new life.

We pray for peace that passes all understanding to garrison their heart and peace in their life.

We pray for the grace to keep them away from the lust of flesh and sustain their trust and honesty.

We pray, let the mercy of God protect their relationships.

We pronounce the grace of God to keep them in wisdom and to live together in harmony, peace and joy.

We pray for the ability to forgive one another and love again.

We pray to God to bind the relationships with the cord that cannot be broken.

We pray to God to grant them understanding.

We pray for the ability to be patient with one another.
In Jesus name, Amen.

MICRO JOURNAL

Dates	

MICRO JOURNAL

Dates	

CHAPTER 7

COMMUNICATION IS THE KEY

Rapport

What we say can create or destroy rapport, but interestingly, the spoken word only makes up 7% of communication.

Our body language and our tone of voice are more important than the actual words spoken.

Have you ever noticed how conversation seems to flow when two people are in rapport?

Their bodies, as well as their words, match each other. Just watch a couple in a restaurant, or friends meeting in a pub; they dance the dance of rapport! Picking up their glasses in unison, matching each other's body language and speaking styles—it's all part of the dance!

So, what is rapport? It is "the process of establishing and maintaining a relationship of mutual trust and understanding between two or more people; the ability to generate responses from another person."

Taken from the book, "Introducing NLP", by Joseph O'Connor & John Seymour.

Non-verbal communication

The ability to communicate non-verbally is a crucial skill to learn and enhance.

Emotions and messages are conveyed through our body language, so this skill is highly visual. Communicate appropriately through the use of facial expressions, gestures, eye contact, body movements, and voice.

Communication supports transparency. The building blocks for matching are body language, posture, weight distribution, gestures, arms and hands, legs and feet, facial expressions, eye contact, and breathing rate, as well as voice quality, volume, tone, pitch, and tempo. Leading enhances rapport by changing the other person's behaviour, by getting them to follow your lead (e.g. leading them from slumping, into a more upright posture, or leading them from speaking quietly to speaking more loudly).

Having rapport and being able to lead others makes it easier to achieve mutually desired outcomes, such as reaching an agreement. If you are prepared to use these skills consciously, you can create rapport with whoever you choose.

You don't have to like the person to create rapport; you are simply building a bridge to understand them better. You will not know that it is effective or what results you'll get unless you try it!

The dance of rapport is what we do naturally. It allows us to join the other person in their model of the world. Rapport needs your flexibility of thought and behaviour. Notice what happens when people get on well—they tend to match. Notice the opposite when people are in disagreement—they mismatch.

Notice when you are not getting on with someone and try matching! Make it easy for others to communicate with you by practising rapport. Liking the other person is not a prerequisite for rapport. For example, if you're having a conflict in a romantic relationship, it helps to hold hands or stay physically connected as you talk. It can remind you that you still care about each other and generally support each other. Keep in mind that it's important to remain respectful of the other person, even if you don't like their actions.

Get comfortable with telling the truth and setting time aside for your relationships.

Sensibly telling the truth about how we feel can benefit a relationship—don't be afraid to communicate the truth to one another, for the truth will build trust and understanding in a relationship. Relationships demand understanding and patience; keep sharing, keep talking, keep listening, keep reasoning, and a peace that passes all understanding will fill your heart.

Creating and honouring time for one another will allow you to understand your differences and appreciate them. There is a saying that the way to a man's heart is through his stomach, but the way to a woman's heart is through her ears—a sacred space, where you set aside time each week to sit without distraction and talk about your relationship is sufficient. Relationships need attention, and the level of attention we give to one another determines the closeness and understanding in our relationships.

Respectful, helpful communication

Giving respect and consideration is essential in a relationship. When partners make each other a priority, respect is a natural eventuality. True love is about putting someone else's needs before your own. Give support rather than undermining the other person. Be considerate and respect their needs, giving time to grow or heal instead of condemning, judging, gossiping, or saying negative words to one another.

Humour brings a lot less tension and a lot more forward motion. Finding the opportunity inside the obstacle is a lesson that carries great weight over time. Nagging and complaining doesn't work; only prayer works. If you prayed more, you'd have a lot less to grumble, complain, nag, and nit-pick about. It's your decision.

Tips on Love communication

- Be mindful of the language you use
- Be sensitive to the words and the present situation
- Be humorous and have fun in your conversation
- Calm when talking
- Tell the truth and be honest
- Keep a clear message
- Know when and where to speak
- Be willing to listen and observe the other person
- Watch your body language
- Watch your tone of voice
- Learn when to stop talking, and know your limits and boundaries
- Let your words carry weight and understanding
- Know the magic words: I'm sorry, thank you, please.
- Avoid unnecessary arguments
- Adopt an attitude of non-judgment
- Do not complain
- Avoid gossip and bad influence
- Speak with respect and dignity

MICRO JOURNAL

Dates	

MICRO JOURNAL

Dates	

CHAPTER 8

TECHNIQUES TO HELP YOU FORGIVE

LET GO, AND MOVE FORWARD WITH GREATER HAPPINESS

1. Think about all the advantages of letting go of your hurt. Make a list of what you would gain by forgiving what has happened to you. Think about how free you would feel. How will your relationship with that person change?

2. List the disadvantages of maintaining your negative feelings. What toll is it taking on you and the people around you? How does it affect your children if you can't forgive your wife, parents, or whomever? Is it going to solve anything by continuing down the path you're currently on?

3. Commit to letting go. It's challenging to accomplish anything without having the intention of doing so. Most people don't miraculously lose 25 pounds or start saving an extra $100 every month; anything positive usually begins with an intention. So commit to finding a way to forgive and move on.

4. Know that you have a choice. We are intelligent, thoughtful creatures. We don't have to simply react to things like lower animals. We have the opportunity to interpret situations and actions we take, before and after the situation occurs. We can also change our minds and choose something different after the initial reaction. WE CHOOSE!

5. Be empathetic. It's easy to assume that the other person is just wrong, but maybe there is more to it than that. What else do they have going on

in their lives? Has something happened in their past that caused them to behave the way that they did? Try to see things from their perspective. You might be surprised at what you find.

6. Consider your part in it. Did you contribute to the issue in some way? It's rare that anyone is 100% innocent when a disagreement occurs. Realising your part in the matter can help you understand your motivations. Also, it's essential to find forgiveness for yourself, as well, if you regret anything that you did or said.

7. Focus on the here and now. Constantly reliving the past just keeps the hurt feelings churning. One of the keys to life is to be in the present. Look around you; what do you see? What are you doing? If you're washing the dishes, be 100% aware of the fact that you're washing the dishes, not thinking about other things. Be present.

8. Move on. Forgive the person, and you'll immediately feel better. We're at our best when we act with compassion. We feel great, too, when compassion and forgiveness are automatically part of our lives. Forgiveness is something that you primarily do for yourself.

We must work on our relationships

It is a fact that love is the foundation of any happy relationship. However, to have a healthy relationship, both parties have to be willing to work on it.

It is not enough to say that we love, but to practice accepting and appreciating others.

We need to understand the fact that our relationships will not be smooth and happy all the time, there will be ups and downs, and we cannot expect everything to be up. No one is perfect, and we should expect to embrace imperfection in our lives and other people's lives, and therefore we should be willing to ride the storms together with better understanding.

Positive and negative experiences

Keep the 3:1 ratio. Over the course of the day, we have a variety of positive and negative experiences. It is also true when it comes to our relationship with our significant other. Most people think that as long as the positive experiences outweigh the negative, everything is fine. However, this isn't so. It's the ratio of positive to negative that matters.

Research has shown that the magical ratio for a flourishing relationship is at or above 3:1. That is, you need to have three times more positive experiences with your partner than negative experiences to have a healthy relationship.

Keep the novelty alive. One of the positive aspects of being in a relationship with someone for a long time is that you get to know each other. The negative side of this is that the novelty wears off, and humans love novelty.

However, there's a way to keep the novelty alive: try new activities together; it creates excitement and uncertainty.

Keep the playfulness alive. We all love to play, regardless of our age. Do the following: have fun together; do something ridiculous together, and just let go. Also, the next time that your partner says something that bothers you try responding with a joke instead.

Focus on the positives.

Dr Terri Orbuch has been conducting a long-term study since 1986 on what makes couples happy and what strengthens relationships. She explains that happy couples focus on what is going well in their relationship, rather than focusing on what is going wrong.

Allow yourself to be vulnerable. Brené Brown, author of "Daring Greatly: How the Courage to Be Vulnerable Transforms the Way We Live, Love, Parent, and Lead", explains that vulnerability holds the key to emotional intimacy. She adds that vulnerability is about being honest with how we feel, about our fears, about what we need, and actually asking for what we need. It's allowing ourselves to be truly seen by our partner, warts and all.

In a nutshell, sometimes life just gets to be a little too much, and it's easy to get overwhelmed, whether it be expectations from your boss, colleagues, friends, family or other half– or even the sky-high expectations you have of yourself. Sometimes we can be left not feeling good enough. In times like these, it can be challenging to gain the perspective we need to pull ourselves out of that terrible slump. Here are things to remember that should get you well on your way to feeling better.

- This too shall pass - As cliché as it sounds, no matter how terrible you feel right now and how desperate your situation may currently seem, it's just a fleeting moment in your life. While it may seem as though your world is ending, trust in the fact that the sun will rise again tomorrow and shine new, hopeful light on you and your predicament.

- No one can do better than you - because there is not a single person out there who is like you! You are blessed with unique attributes that make comparing yourself to anyone else, not only futile and discouraging but also, quite frankly, impossible. No one has lived the life you've lived, so no one is better equipped to tackle your challenges than you. Remember this whenever you catch your subconscious trying to convince you that you are not as worthy as someone else!

- This challenge will only make you stronger - Even though you may feel broken and bruised now, you will recover from this ordeal a more resilient person. When we get injured, the scar tissue that develops to mend our damaged skin is more durable than you could ever imagine. It's the same for your heart and soul: trust in their ability to heal, too.

- Celebrate your failures; they are a lesson - As the wonderful Oprah Winfrey says, "Think like a queen. A queen is not afraid to fail. Failure is another step to greatness." When terrible things happen (either of our own doing or otherwise), it can be difficult to see the forest for the trees. However, in every failure or negative moment, there is a lesson to be learned. Take heart, and have faith in the fact that thanks to this experience, you will be better equipped to deal with whatever life throws at you next.

- You're good enough to try, and that's all you need to do - now that you know that failures should be celebrated and not feared, the time has come to realise that everything you've accomplished up until now and everything you'll achieve comes from you taking a leap of faith and trying. No matter how convinced you are that you are going to fail, attempt it.

- Progress trumps perfection, every time - It is so easy to get caught up in others' expectations that we forget that perfection is an unrealistic (and frankly, boring) ideal. By shooting for perfection, you are setting yourself up for feeling like rubbish when you inevitably fall short. Progress, on the other hand, is a better measure of how brilliant you are and how much you've grown. Celebrate every small step forward.

- You are not alone - Although insecurity tends to confine us to a very lonely place, know that there are people around you who are desperate to show you how amazing you are and how much you matter. Even if you can't see your worth right now, they most certainly can; and while you may feel like you're burdening them by expressing your feelings, I can assure you they don't see it that way. Remember that even when you don't feel good enough, your friends and relatives think you're the bee's knees. Don't be afraid to reach out.

- Everyone is fighting a hard battle - While your problem is deeply personal and unique to your situation, take comfort in the fact that others are also feeling less than great. It is not, of course, so that you can take pleasure from their pain, but because this means you are not alone in your plight. No matter how desperate you may feel, there is someone out there who will be able to relate and bring solace. All you need to do is find them. There is so much to be thankful for - When I'm down, one thing I like to do is list three things that I am grateful for, right in the moment. It is an excellent exercise for gaining perspective: even though it may feel like the world is crashing down around me, being able to make a gratitude list reminds me that there is a silver lining. Give it a try–you'll be surprised at the results.

Here is a short exercise, where I want you to list all the things you are grateful for in your relationships, this could be with your spouse, children, friends, extended family; even strangers you have met this week.

What and who am I grateful for this week?

The next question I want you to ask yourself is: What am I grateful for in myself?

A note: You are deserving of love - You may feel terrible about yourself now, but I can guarantee that there is so much beauty in you. In times when you don't feel good enough, name three things that you love about yourself. If you're having trouble with coming up with something, be grateful for your lungs, which allow you to breathe; your mouth, which helps you to smile; your soul, which makes you, you.

You are a thing of wonder; believe it! Your mind can be cruel; don't always take it at its word - We are often our very worst critics. Even if we are kind to others, it can be hard for us to be kind to ourselves.
We tend to judge ourselves extremely harshly, whether we're aware of it or not, simply because we're conditioned by society to believe we need to look or behave a certain way. When we don't conform to these impossible standards, it's easy to slip into negative self-talk. Be aware of this and don't believe everything you think.

So I will ask again: What are you grateful for in yourself?

You have a choice - Now that you know your subconscious isn't always your best friend, it's time to understand that you have a choice. You could choose to let that nagging voice of discord run its mouth, or you could decide to fake it until you make it and replace your negative thoughts with positive ones.

All it takes is the resolve to wear those rose-tinted glasses (no matter how cheesy it may feel at first) and practice! Commit to it, and I promise you'll feel a change. Your approval is the only one that matters - We spend our lives bending over backwards trying to please others, trying to conform to others' ideas and we lose sight of what matters: our happiness and fulfilment. People come and go, but you're stuck with yourself for the rest of your life. Do yourself a favour and focus on how you feel about yourself before worrying about the others. I'll bet that once you strip away others' expectations, you'll like what you see.

You have overcome so much already - You may feel terrible now, but remember how much you've already achieved. Think about the path that has led you to where you are now. Reminisce about your life from an objective perspective and see how much you've accomplished and overcome. Even though it may not seem like it now, you are a warrior, and you are capable of so much. You are still giving it your all - even when life knocks you down, you'll always be there fighting. The fact that you feel the way you do right now is an indication that you still care and you still want to succeed. You haven't given up, and that means so much more than you realise.

There is always a way to get unstuck - No matter how desperate the situation, there's still something you can do to move forward. You may not see it in the moment, but you will uncover it eventually, either on your own or with the help of your friends. In that "aha" moment, you'll come to realise how close you were to the solution all along. Hindsight is always 20/20, isn't it? Don't lose hope; the answer you're seeking is out there.

You are in no hurry - Just because everybody else is running ragged doesn't mean that you need to hold yourself to the same, crazy standards. The most significant goals and achievements in life take time to accomplish. Don't pressure yourself into getting everything done too quickly and get down on yourself when you don't quite manage it. It's okay to take a little longer and savour the process.

It's okay not to be okay - Sometimes, you need to surrender to your feelings and allow yourself to not be Superman or Superwoman for once. The world will carry on turning without you holding it together. Give yourself permission to give in to your emotions and know that it's okay to give yourself a break. You've worked so hard–you deserve it. No matter how dark the clouds above your head, there are better days right around the corner. Believe in yourself, give yourself a break, and you will get there.

Finally, Prayer works, prayer form the preparation, it makes things work in relationship when you pray together, it unites husband and wife to build famly, prayer iin the midst of storm gives the insurance that all will be well and no condition is pernament. Prayer is the key above all phylosopies and principles.

Wisdom is the principlar thing and in our getting, get understanding. When you understand life, you will get wisdom to practice then you pray to water and nurtue the relationship daily.

The mapping of 'I Can Love Again'

I- Inspiration.

C- Communication.

A- Accountability.

N- Nurture.

L- Live your life.

O- Overcome obstacles.

V- Value yourself.

E- Enjoy life.

A- Acknowledge one another.

G- Gain knowledge.

A- Action.

I- Ignite the fire.

N- New Beginnings.

The Love We Lost

MICRO JOURNAL

Dates	

MICRO JOURNAL

Dates	

CHAPTER 9

THE STRATEGY OF LOVE

Personal SWOT Analysis

A personal SWOT analysis is an excellent tool for evaluating yourself and your life in general, or for a specific aspect that you may want to change. It helps you think things through, get a more balanced perspective, and then consider what to do next. SWOT stands for Strengths, Weaknesses, Opportunities and Threats. You may be familiar with its use in business, yet you can apply it to your personal life too.

How to Use SWOT - Get a piece of paper (preferably A4 or bigger). Write down, what you are reviewing as a title to help you stay focussed. Then divide the paper into quarters. Draw a line across the page halfway down from the top and halfway down from the side.

The top two rectangles are for focusing on the current, often internal, aspects of SWOT, the strengths and weaknesses. You then enter the lower two sections with the possibilities and risks available, labelling them as opportunities and threats.

Strengths

For a personal SWOT analysis, the strengths are everything good about you. For example, you can list specific skills, experience, flexibilities, willingness to re-train and so on. If the analysis is about a personal situation, such as your relationship with someone, you will list the good points pertinent to the relationship – the good times you've had together, shared interests, how you help each other.

Weaknesses

Weaknesses are where the problems lie, either with you or the situation. For instance, if you had to make a job change that may highlight your need to stay near an ageing parent or that you may lack a required qualification. A SWOT analysis of a relationship may list poor communication as a weakness.

Opportunities

Opportunities are things that haven't happened; you may or may not have noticed them. It is your chance to identify and think them through. Whom do you know that could help you get a new job? What courses are available? Would counselling help your relationship improve or perhaps just making more time for each other? *Use this section to explore all possibilities, even if they seem far-fetched.*

Threats

Threats are also things that haven't happened but could hamper the success of what you want to do. When considering a job change, you might hate the new company or role or the job may not last. For your relationship, threats are the chance you may grow apart; your partner may meet someone else. Although this is a cynical exercise, it is still important. As with the opportunities, use your imagination to try to envisage many avenues.

Using Your Personal SWOT Analysis

As you complete your SWOT analysis, you may find some sections harder to complete than others. Give yourself time, leave it and come back to it later if that helps. Sometimes one or more of the areas will have less in it than the others. The thinking behind the SWOT analysis is what counts. It allows you to take a more balanced view of the situation. Once you believe you have completed it as well as you can, you can then consider your next steps.

SWOT Analysis Template

Strength	

Weakness	

Opportunities	

Threats	

The Love We Lost

Likes and Dislike

Likes	Dislike

Similarities and Differences

Similarities	Differences

The Love We Lost

What do you know about Man and Woman

About Man	About Woman

Let us categorize behaviour of couples into different kinds of relationship patterns during Conflicts

How they resolve conflicts	How they avoid conflicts	How they escalate conflicts	How they manage and work through conflict

The Love We Lost

About Your Spouse

Assess the Situation

Your impact in the situation

MICRO JOURNAL

Dates	

MICRO JOURNAL

Dates	

CHAPTER 10

LOVE QUOTES

Let us always meet each other with a smile as the smile is the beginning of love. Mother Teresa

Keep love in your hearts; a life without it is like a sunless garden when the flowers are dead. Oscar Wilde

What we have once enjoyed we can never lose. All that we love deeply becomes a part of us. Helen Keller

One is loved because one is loved; no reason is needed for loving.
Paulo Coelho

Life without love is like a tree without blossoms or fruit. Khalil Gibran

A new command I give you: love one another as I have loved you; you must love one another. Jesus Christ.

The hunger for love is much more difficult to remove than the hunger for bread. Mother Teresa.

The love we have in our youth is superficial compared to the love that an old man has for his wife. Will Durant

A man is already halfway in love with any woman who listens to him.
Breida Behan

The Love We Lost

With our love, we could save the world.
George Harrison

The richest love is that which submits to the arbitration of time.
Lawrence Durrell

Be strong, but not rude; be kind but not weak; be bold but not bully.
Jim Rohn

If you want to maintain your values and principles in life, especially now, be careful who you call friends for many have fallen from grace because they are surrounded by compromisers who live by preference, not principle. Elizabeth Lucas-Afolalu

Love is the greatest investment.
Elizabeth Lucas-Afolalu

You cannot walk away from the love you have spent quality time to build for many years. Elizabeth Lucas-Afolalu

Forgiveness frees you from bitterness and makes you happy.
Elizabeth Lucas-Afolalu

Nothing will change until you are willing to change.
Elizabeth Lucas-Afolalu

You need to think right if you want to build more meaningful relationships. Elizabeth Lucas-Afolalu

There is divine protection and honour in serving others with love and humility. Elizabeth Lucas-Afolalu

Forgiveness will release you into greatness, forgive yourself and forgive others, yes you can. Elizabeth Lucas-Afolalu

Yes, you can love again.
Elizabeth Lucas-Afolalu

Your mindset has to change for you to experience transformation in your relationship. Elizabeth Lucas-Afolalu

Love is everything; love is relationship, business, family, wealth, and future. Elizabeth Lucas-Afolalu

Love is the greatest it conquers, protects, and heals.
Elizabeth Lucas-Afolalu

Forget the past, forgive yourself and others and press forward, the future is bright. Elizabeth Lucas-Afolalu

Love is such a simple, beautiful word. If only being in love was that easy! Instead, it is a complicated, ever-changing jumble of feelings and emotions. Jennifer Fox

Love is a special gift that you can give over and over again and is completely within your power. How you treat people, how you react when you are upset, how you listen, how you share, these are all ways we can demonstrate love for others. Catherine Pulsifer

Love is a mighty power, a great and complete good. Love alone lightens every burden and makes rough places smooth. It bears every hardship as though it were nothing, and renders all bitterness sweet and acceptable. Thomas A Kempis

To have joy is to have love, love is the result of peace, longsuffering, goodness, honesty, discipline and trust. Elizabeth Lucas-Afolalu.

Actions speak louder than thoughts – it's what you do when presented with the opportunity that showcases your love, or lack of" Anna Shine.

We grow in love by choosing to serve, share, listen, forgive, etc. Love grows as we choose to act in love towards others. Gregory Brown

There is no greater gift you can give yourself than to love freely and with your whole heart. Carolyn Robinson

Improving communication is essential for a better understanding. Elizabeth Lucas-Afolalu.

Desire to become better in life by changing your mindset; set goals, take actions and get better. Elizabeth Lucas-Afolalu

You are so special; you are unique, be happy, stay joyful stay blessed and highly favoured. Elizabeth Lucas-Afolalu

Trials and tribulations May come your way, discouragement and disappointment may try to pull you down but don't give up, don't quit, for you are the next on the list, to be remembered and to be favoured. Elizabeth Lucas-Afolalu

The truth is, no condition is permanent. Elizabeth Lucas-Afolalu

Failure does not classify you as inferior, but it means you are not perfect and are willing to change for the better. Elizabeth Lucas-Afolalu

In every challenge of life, there is always a way out, and in every problem, there is a solution. Elizabeth Lucas-Afolalu

The Love We Lost

Yes, you can go after what you want and get it, take up anything and improve it, take any situation, turn it around and make it work for you. Elizabeth Lucas-Afolalu

Love requires, listening to one another, overcoming together, valuing one another and enjoying together. Elizabeth Lucas-Afolalu

The level of your passion is the level of your determination.
 Elizabeth Lucas-Afolalu

 Situations and circumstances will make you stronger, even if it feels difficult as it might sometimes be. It could be an excellent opportunity for you to succeed and grow. Elizabeth Lucas-Afolalu

The truth is, there is a life force within each person; look inside and discover yourself. Elizabeth Lucas-Afolalu

The first step to getting somewhere is to decide that you're not going to stay where you are. Elizabeth Lucas-Afolalu

Stretch yourself to new heights, there's no limit to how high you can go. Elizabeth Lucas-Afolalu

You can not judge things from a distance because you will tell lies or half-truths. Elizabeth Lucas-Afolalu

Avoid bowing down to the challenges you are facing now because they are not there to destroy you but to prepare you for greatness. Elizabeth Lucas-Afolalu

Think not that you can not do something before you try it because you really can love again. Elizabeth Lucas-Afolalu

The Love We Lost

You are bigger than any situation you are facing right now.
Elizabeth Lucas-Afolalu

You have the gifts, talents and skills to make life worth living, use them.
Elizabeth Lucas-Afolalu

The future is brighter than how you perceive it now.
Elizabeth Lucas-Afolalu

You cannot make anyone love you, but love yourself and let yourselves be loved. Elizabeth Lucas-Afolalu

What is most valuable is not what you have in your lives but whom you have in your lives. Elizabeth Lucas-Afolalu

Stop comparing you to others; all will be judged individually on their own merits. Elizabeth Lucas-Afolalu

A rich person is not the one who has the most but is the one who shares what he has. Elizabeth Lucas-Afolalu

It only takes a few seconds to open profound wounds in people we love, and it takes many years to heal them, to forgive is by practising forgiveness. Elizabeth Lucas-Afolalu

It is not changing location that matters but changing your mindset that will make you succeed. Elizabeth Lucas-Afolalu

For God so loved the world that He gave his only begotten son that whosoever believe in him will not perish but have eternal life. John 3:16
The Greatest Book

The Love We Lost

Truth is they love you dearly, but they simply do not know how to express or show their feelings. Elizabeth Lucas-Afolalu

Two people can look at the same thing and see it differently. Elizabeth Lucas-Afolalu

A true friend is someone who knows everything about you and likes you anyway. Elizabeth Lucas-Afolalu

It is not always enough that you been forgiven by others; forgive yourself. Elizabeth Lucas-Afolalu

People will forget what you said, People will forget what you did, People will forget what you wear or how you look, but people will never forget how you made them feel, be an impact. Elizabeth Lucas-Afolalu

Unforgiveness kills a relationship and brings bitterness. Elizabeth Lucas-Afolalu

Forgiveness is not optional but mandatory; it is essential to press forward.
Elizabeth Lucas-Afolalu

If you make a mess, clean it up and do not wait for someone else to take responsibility. Elizabeth Lucas-Afolalu

When you disappoint those close to you, resist the urge to make excuses or blame others; take responsibility for your actions and ask for forgiveness. Elizabeth Lucas-Afolalu

Do not compromise your faith or your values to follow the crowd. The crowd might be wrong. Elizabeth Lucas-Afolalu

Do not pretend to be who you're not nor hide from your true self, and also do not hide your faith or your beliefs from others.
Elizabeth Lucas-Afolalu

You will be tempted as you've never been tempted before. It takes character and determination not to succumb to these temptations. Tap into it every time the need arises. Elizabeth Lucas-Afolalu

You can only unite when you show love and forgive, tolerate and understand others. Elizabeth Lucas-Afolalu

Assess your thinking, is it productive; constructive; creative; inventive and positive? For what you are thinking will reflect your life.
Elizabeth Lucas-Afolalu

If it is going to be, it is up to you, do something.
Elizabeth Lucas-Afolalu

Our weapons are not guns and knives, but spiritual. Go on your knees and pray. Elizabeth Lucas-Afolalu

A mature man will walk away and let peace reign.
Elizabeth Lucas-Afolalu

Argument and violence will not solve the problem of tension but will pollute and damage the atmosphere. Elizabeth Lucas-Afolalu

Be happy and stay blessed.
Elizabeth Lucas-Afolalu

Trials and tribulations may come your way, how you deal with it matters.
Elizabeth Lucas-Afolalu

The Love We Lost

Discouragement and disappointment may try to pull you down, Hold on and be strong. Elizabeth Lucas-Afolalu

Be patient, be prayerful, be smart, be positive, be happy and be blessed. Elizabeth Lucas-Afolalu

Keep up the excellent works for in due season you shall reap and enjoy what you have sown. Elizabeth Lucas-Afolalu

The world is waiting for you to use your gift to solve a problem. Elizabeth Lucas-Afolalu

 You have something extraordinary that only YOU are capable of bringing to life and sharing with the world. Elizabeth Lucas-Afolalu

Learn to live above the opinions of others around you and not worry about what anyone else thinks or says about you. Elizabeth Lucas-Afolalu

Focus on your self, focus on your purpose.
Elizabeth Lucas-Afolalu

Focus on everything that matters to you.
Elizabeth Lucas-Afolalu

Focus on what you have, use it and share with others
 Elizabeth Lucas-Afolalu

Focus on your destination. You must have a clear picture of where you want to go in life, press in and don't look back at yesterday.
Matthew Ashimolowo

Embrace your imperfection and our differences and respect other people's values. Elizabeth Lucas-Afolalu

The Love We Lost

Don't let the p[inions of other destroy your happiness and hold you back.
Elizabeth Lucas-Afolalu

Love is the greatest Investment in life.
Elizabeth Lucas-Afolalu

MICRO JOURNAL

Dates	

MICRO JOURNAL

Dates	

The Love We Lost

ABOUT THE AUTHOR

Elizabeth Lucas-Afolalu is the Award-Winning Author, Inspirational Speaker, Family and relationship Adviser, and Youth mentor.

She has been recognised for her contributions to Humanity and Community. She has been awarded, Author of Greatness, Woman of Excellence, The Legend Award for Humanity, Inspiration and Relationship Award, Humanity Award, Ambassador Shine Award, Award-Winning author of Yes You Can, Award-Winning Speaker (for WAGES NGO and Advocate for Young Ladies), Secretary of the Year.

She has been featured on National Press such as Financial Herald, Fox, ABC and NBC, Small business Trendsetter magazine, Okunsgroup Magazine, Powerhouse Global Magazine and Local Hornchurch Newspaper. She has also been involving in Charities/NGO including Great Osmond Children Hospital, Children Deaf association, Salvation Army and CFAN, British Heart Foundation and Friends of Dementia.

She is an International Speaker at Powerhouse Dubai Summit 2020 and Global Woman Business London Summit and Global Woman Business Summit. She shares her wisdom, incredible personal story and experiences. She has set up a programme to help Youth, Women and Families in the area of Renewing Mindset, Building Relationships, Creating Kingdom Wealth and Personal Development in her Yes You Can Online Academy.

She is the founder of many businesses including Tokmez Limited, Elizabeth Kreations, Yes You Can Online Academy, Yes you Can feel Good, look Good and Be Happy. Tokmez Publishing, Time with Elizabeth Lucas Inspiration/Mentoring, and Partner to many Organisations. She is Co-Author of two books, "Jesus Saves Our Lives" with Professor Patrick Businge, and "Tough Roads Create Tough People" with Lady Anita Bradshaw.

The Love We Lost

Other books written by Elizabeth Lucas-Afolalu

1. Yes You Can: Build Deeper Relationship; Earn more money and be a happier you

2. Yes You Can Mindset 101

3. Inspirational Nuggets of Wisdom

The Love We Lost

YES YOU CAN

Do you think you could become, be, and do much more than you are doing now?

Do you need motivation and help to develop perseverance to pursue your life goals?

Do you want to develop the mindset that will push you to improve your character traits, which will lead you to unlimited success in life?

Do you want to have a healthy relationship and be happy? Perhaps, you are not showing up as much as you know you should.

Or you suffer worry and anxiety about being visible on social media, in person, or anywhere else.

Or you need help to overcome low self-esteem and lack of confidence.

And you want support to step into your power show up and show off.

I have created something very special to help you. I offer 30 minutes free consultation of Yes, You Can Life Coaching in areas of Relationship, Empowerment, Personal Development, and Success.

I have many years of experience of mentoring and inspiring and advising individuals, youths and families ascribing for success, and there are positive results and testimonies, including testimonial, relationship restored, my life experience and wisdom which I have uploaded and downloaded into a system.

Visit www.yesyoucan-by-elizabeth.com

The Love We Lost

ELIZABETH KREAATIONS
Inspirational Gifts, Resources and Digital Products

There are wide range of Inspirational Gifts, Resources and Digital products including latest books by Elizabeth Lucas-Afolalu in the Web store. - A collection of inspirational and motivational gifts and resources that give us the courage to pursue our life's dreams and goals, and that have the power to even get us through a bad week.

Our gift shop is known for providing highly inspiring, innovative, and humorous gifts, stylish home décor, and desirable collectables. You can also have your item personalised for that special person or for yourself.

We have an excellent collection of highly inspirational stories, articles, videos, and other materials that leave you deeply inspired to be all that you can be, and all are available to order from our website. Creating a library of inspirational resources is a vital way to increase your spiritual growth and have valuable insight into God's Word.

Visit: www.elizabethkreations.co.uk

Thank you.

The Love We Lost

The Love We Lost

www.ingramcontent.com/pod-product-compliance
Lightning Source LLC
Chambersburg PA
CBHW050830160426
43192CB00010B/1971